How to Lavish a Leo

a Leo

Real Life Guidance on How to
Get Along and Be Friends with
the 5th Sign of the Zodiac

WHAT PEOPLE ARE SAYING ABOUT

HOW TO LAVISH A LEO

"This light-hearted and delightfully lively look into the inner workings of Leo provides ample tips on how to make your big cat purr with pride and pleasure."
Pauline Edward, Astrologer, author of *Astrological Crosses in Relationships*

"What a great insight into the Leo character! I learnt a lot about myself, and my Leo friends that I didn't know before. I liked all the case studies too. Mary has a nice way of making it more personal instead of text-book like."
Hannah Murray, presenter *Talk Radio Europe*

How to Lavish a Leo

Real Life Guidance on How to
Get Along and Be Friends with
the 5th Sign of the Zodiac

Mary English

Winchester, UK
Washington, USA

First published by Dodona Books, 2013
Dodona Books is an imprint of John Hunt Publishing Ltd., Laurel House, Station Approach,
Alresford, Hants, SO24 9JH, UK
office1@jhpbooks.net
www.johnhuntpublishing.com
www.dodona-books.com

For distributor details and how to order please visit the 'Ordering' section on our website.

Text copyright: Mary English 2013

ISBN: 978 1 78099 977 7

A CIP catalogue record for this book is available from the British Library.

Design: Stuart Davies

Printed and bound by CPI Group (UK) Ltd, Croydon, CR0 4YY

We operate a distinctive and ethical publishing philosophy in all areas of our business, from our global network of authors to production and worldwide distribution.

CONTENTS

Also by Mary English

6 Easy Steps in Astrology
The Birth Charts of Indigo Children
How to Survive a Pisces (O-Books)
How to Bond with an Aquarius (O-Books)
How to Cheer Up a Capricorn (O-Books)
How to Believe in a Sagittarius (O-Books)
How to Win the Trust of a Scorpio (Dodona Books)
How to Love a Libra (Dodona Books)
How to Soothe a Virgo (Dodona Books)
How to Listen to a Gemini (Dodona Books)
How to Satisfy a Taurus (Dodona Books)
How to Appreciate an Aries (Dodona Books)

Please visit Mary's site at www.maryenglish.com

This book is dedicated to Wally
May You Rest in the Arms of Angels in Heaven.

Acknowledgements

I would like to thank the following people:

My son for being the Libran that makes me always look on the other side.

My Taurus husband Jonathan for being the most wonderful man in my world.

Mabel, Jessica and Usha for their Homeopathic help and understanding.

Laura and Mandy for their friendship.

Donna Cunningham for all her help and advice.

Judy Hall for her inspiration.

Alois Treindl for being the Pisces that founded the wonderful Astro.com website.

Judy Ramsell Howard at the Bach Centre for her encouragement.

John my publisher for being the person that fought tooth and nail to get this book published and all the staff at O-Books including Stuart, Nick, Trevor, Kate, Catherine, Elizabeth, the two Maria's and Mary.

Louise Knapper for her wonderful title suggestion.

Mary Shukle, Alam, Oksana and Christine for their helpful read-throughs.

And last but not least my lovely clients for their valued contributions.

Introduction

I started this series of Astrology books with *How to Survive a Pisces*, about my sign and after the book had been accepted at the publisher's (who is, I found out later, a Pisces!) he told me he didn't just want one book. Ooooh, I thought, I'd better write one for each sign of the Zodiac. And as there are 12 signs of the Zodiac I then realised I'd got quite a lengthy project.

Being an Astrologer is a funny life. I was writing *How to Soothe a Virgo* when I caught myself hanging out the duvet on the washing line, trying to line-up the seams so that it would be perfectly straight and not need so much ironing. I was busy lining-up the hems when I thought to myself, 'This is a very Virgo thing, needing so much perfection.'

When I started writing this book on Leos, I was involved in the on-going sceptical attack against Homeopaths and Homeopathy, and I again caught myself just after I'd written a letter to HRH The Prince of Wales to get his support for an Act of Parliament that was going through.

I didn't even think that there was any problem writing to a member of the Royal Family (who I have never met, or am never likely to!) and it wasn't until I'd popped the letter in the letter-box over the road, that I thought, 'That was a very Leo thing to do, to contact the Royal Family!' and there lies the theme of Leo: acting like Royalty. I had a little chuckle to myself. It was as if I were 'proving'* each sign as I wrote about it.

A proving is a Homeopathic method of finding a remedy's healing function, by having volunteers sample a dose and record their experiences.

Before we learn about Leo, we need to discover a little about Astrology and where it came from and where it is today. It's been around for a long time and most cultures have some connection with the soul or the spirit. They observe the planets, the Sun and Moon and have made a correlation between our place here on Earth, and the Gods' place in 'heaven above'.

A Brief History of Astrology

Christopher McIntosh, a historian, tells us in his *The Astrologers and Their Creed* that Astrology was discovered in what is now called the Middle East: Iraq:

It was the priests of the kingdom of Babylonia who made the discovery, which set the pattern for the development of astronomy and of the zodiacal system of astrology that we know today. For many generations they had been meticulously observing and recording the movements of the heavenly bodies. Finally they had, by careful calculation, discovered that there were besides the Sun and the Moon five other visible planets which moved in established courses through the sky. These were the planets that we now call Mercury, Venus, Mars, Jupiter and Saturn.

The discovery which these priest-astronomers made was a remarkable one, considering how crude were the instruments with which they worked. They had no telescopes, nor any of the complicated apparatus, which astronomers use today. But they did have one big advantage. The area, next to the Persian Gulf, on which their kingdom lay, was blessed with extremely clear skies. In order to make full use of this advantage they built towers on flat areas of country and from these were able to scan the entire horizon.

These priests lived highly secluded lives in monasteries usually adjacent to the towers. Every day they observed the movements of the heavenly spheres and noted down any corresponding earthly phenomena from floods to rebellions. Very early on they had come to the conclusion that the laws which governed the movements of the stars and planets also governed events on Earth. The seasons changed with the movements of the Sun, therefore, they argued, the other heavenly bodies must surely exercise a similar influence....

In the beginning the stars and planets were regarded as being actual gods. Later, as religion became more sophisticated, the two ideas were separated and the belief developed that the god 'ruled' the corresponding planet.

Gradually, a highly complex system was built up in which each planet had a particular set of properties ascribed to it. This system was developed partly through the reports of the priests and partly through the natural characteristics of the planets. Mars was seen to be red in colour and was therefore identified with the god Nergal, the fiery god of war and destruction.

Venus, identified by the Sumerians as their goddess Inanna, was the most prominent in the morning, giving birth, as it were, to the day. She therefore became the planet associated with the female qualities of love, gentleness and reproduction.

The observation of the stars by the Sumerians was mostly a religious act. The planets were their gods and each visible object was associated with an invisible spiritual being that judged their actions, blessed them with good fortune or sent them tribulations.[1]

Astrology was therefore born out of careful observation and also a desire by the Sumerians to add meaning to their lives. As first it was for a practical purpose, to help their crops; then it developed into one that was spiritual. Astrology then worked its way across vast continents until it reached us here in the West and thousands of years later, Astrology is still with us.

So, here we are at Leo. The sign of the lion. The regal sign of the lion as Leo is not just any old lion, they are THE LION!

Grrrr!! How did it get these characteristics? Where did they come from?

This is what we will learn about in this book, and hopefully you will understand what is important to a Leo and how to make living, loving or being with a Leo the wonderful experience it should be.

Mary English

Bath

June 2012

Chapter One

The Sign

I believe that the Principle which gives life dwells in us and without us comes from the Supreme Intelligence through the Rays of the Sun.
Alan Leo

Leo is the fifth sign of the Zodiac. To call someone a Leo they would have to be born between a certain set of dates that are generally 23rd July to 23rd August. I say generally as it does depend where in the world you were born and also what time of day. And if you were born during those dates mentioned above, you would really need to check with a good astrological programme or Astrologer to make sure your Leo actually is a Leo.

If they were born very early on the morning of the 23rd July, the Sun might not have quite changed sign into Leo, and you might have a Cancer on your hands.

No need to worry though, as we're going to use a reliable Swiss Astrological website that Astrologers use.

Each sign of the Zodiac has a planet that 'looks after' it, we call it their 'ruler' and the ruler to Leo is the Sun.

That vast ball of burning flame that we can see in the sky is connected spiritually (not literally) with our friend the lion.

The Enormous Burning Star

If I had to choose a religion, the sun as the universal giver of life would be my god.
Napoleon Bonaparte

In astrology, we call all the celestial beings 'planets' which isn't

5

technically correct. The Sun is actually a star, and while there are thousands of millions of other stars in our own Milky Way, our Sun is special because we depend on it for our survival. It provides us with heat and light, which are rather necessary things for us on Earth. Imagine what life would be like if it was cold all the time and dark. No plants would be able to grow because they depend on light to convert carbon dioxide into oxygen via photosynthesis... and if there was no oxygen, we'd all be dead in less than 10 minutes. Not a fun thought is it?

So for us, the Sun is jolly important.

The Sun is called a 'great powerhouse' because it is like a giant nuclear furnace. It is 1,392,000 km across its diameter, big enough to swallow up our Earth a million times, and produces 7,000 million tons of hydrogen every second. This enormous energy release makes our Sun shine and it's been doing this for more than 4.5 billion years and hopefully will continue to do so for a similar length of time.[2]

The Sun isn't actually yellow. This is an illusion as it's really an enormous white ball of gas with no solid edge, with a temperature of 5,500° C. Astronomers think the temperature at its core could be 15,000,000°C. Bit too hot for sunbathing!

There's a lot going on, with sunspots and solar activity and things called 'coronal mass ejections' hurling electrically charged particles out into space. These cause the celestial light shows called northern and southern lights when they hit the Earth, but too many of them can pose a threat to satellite electronics and power grids.

Like everything, too much of a good thing can be a problem.

I asked a few Leos about their thoughts on the Sun. Here is Helena, a young 30 year old English lady who works for a media company in Portugal:

I couldn't live without the sun. It makes EVERYTHING better! I go a nice caramel brown, and feel sooo happy when the sun is out. After living in Portugal, I would struggle living in the UK again, purely because of lack of sun!

Clarissa is a full-time Mom who lives and works in Canada:

I love the sun as far as lifting my spirits – I can achieve a nice tan but also have to be careful to not burn.

Laura is in her late 20s and lives and works in New Zealand as a graphic designer:

I love the sun. I like to be warm. I dislike being cold or wet, prefer warm/dry. I have fair skin and don't tan easily. Summer is my favorite time of year.

I feel like I have more energy when it is sunny and happier. I like red sunsets especially over water.

Julie is in her 70s and lives in middle England and is a housewife. She loves the sun too:

I love the sun, I am out in it all the time. I have my meals outside. The windows and doors open wide so the fresh air can come in. I am fair skinned but have a good tan. The sun makes me feel charged up.

Margaret is a holistic practitioner and lives in the USA:

I am not sun sensitive and I tan nicely. I've always loved the sun and thrive on it. To me it feels that I am alive, it makes me happy and I can be outside. The sun is our life giver and I feel it gives me life. If it gets humid I deal with it. I could call myself a sun worshipper in a sense that I just love the sun, not that I lay outside all day to get a tan, which I don't do. Without the sun we would have no life.

Only one of the people I asked wasn't quite as positive about our burning star. Diane is an Astrologer and lives in South Wales:

I don't like the hot weather, I burn easily and so avoid sitting out when it is very sunny.

Notice, how all of them (except Diane) have in their answers 'I love the Sun'.

I remember my lovely Leo nephew, who used to live in Bristol, bemoaning the lack of Sun here in the West Country. Our weather is very temperate, a bit like Irish weather and we do have lots of rain, which is why it's so green here. But he was getting depressed that the Sun hadn't been out much and eventually he moved abroad.

The Sun is such a majestic and magnificent planet (remember it's actually a Star) it can't fail to have an influence on our friend the Leo who was born during the Summer months, when the Sun is at its zenith.

Qualities and Element

Each sign of the Zodiac has a quality and element that describes it. Leo is a 'Fixed' quality, doesn't like change, prefers things to stay the same (with them being worshipped and loved) and likes certain things without much alteration. Its Element is 'Fire' (more of this at the end of this chapter).

So what other qualities do astrologers say that Leo has?

Let's ask Colin Evans in *The New Waite's Compendium of Natal Astrology*, 1967:

This sign is of the element Fire, and of fixed quality. Leo individuals are proud, passionate, ambitious, masterful, honourable, irrepressible, delighting in all that is really big in life.[3]

Here is Linda Goodman in her *Sun signs:*

These men and women never lean on others. Instead, they prefer to be leaned on. Responsibility towards the weak and helpless appeals to them. Leo may roar theatrically that everyone depends on him and he's forced to carry the whole load, but don't pay a bit of attention to his complaints. He loves it. Try to relieve him of his burdens or lend a helping hand, and you'll see how quickly Leo will disdainfully refuse your help.[4]

How about asking AT Mann (who is a Leo) in his: *The Round Art: The Astrology of Time and Place*:

Leo governs Self-consciousness, pride, the affections, love of the self and others, creation, acting, confidence... self-glorification, leadership, courage, extroversion, fun-loving, arrogant...[5]

Here is Christopher McIntosh in his book *Astrology, the Stars and Human Life: A Modern Guide* in 1970:

The person born with his Sun in Leo is almost invariably a strong personality with a taste for leadership. The sign has always been associated with monarchs and rulers. The faults than can afflict the sign are conceit, vanity, pomposity, and a lust for power. At his best, however, the Leonian is a thoroughly likeable person, warm, and out-going, with a great capacity to attract the friendship, loyalty, and respect of others.[6]

What does Rae Orion say in *Astrology for Dummies*?

The sunny side
You've got flair. If you're a typical Leo, you are generous, outgoing, loyal and likeable (most of the time)...
The sorry side
Beneath your flamboyant personality, you would be humiliated if anyone ever knew how hard you try or how vulnerable you actually

are. You desperately want people to like you...[7]

What about Marion D. March and Joan McEvers in their *The Only Way to Learn Astrology*:

Key phrase I will... dramatic, idealistic, proud, creative, dignified, generous, self-assured, optimistic, vain, boastful, pretentious.[8]

Here is another astrological team. Felix Lyle and Bryan Aspland in *The Instant Astrologer* say:

self-assured, sincere, generous, optimistic, constant, dignified, spontaneous... also arrogant, intolerant, sloppy, demonstrative, domineering, self-obsessed, pompous, lazy and autocratic.[9]

I think we can safely say that the main keywords for a Leo personality are warm and demonstrative, dramatic, optimistic and vain.

Warm and Demonstrative

There is no doubt that being warm and demonstrative are typical Leo traits. They are playful and childlike (not childish, see below) qualities and make being with a Leo fun rather than draining.

Leos love to show their affection by buying carefully thought-out gifts. Here are a few examples:

Here is Laura again:

Best presents I have given people have been things that came from the heart, like paintings I have done for friends just because I knew they would enjoy the surprise.

One Leo lady I asked had a very simple answer:

The children's first pony.

Margaret also likes to give things she has made:

Being able to give things that are unexpected, handmade or bought, to family and friends and see their surprised faces.

Jenny is a Virgo and an author and is married, second-time round, to a Leo. She talks about her husband Patrick:

He's one of the most caring men I've ever met. He'll go far out of his way to help a friend. You've heard the saying: 'He's in touch with his feminine side.' Patrick definitely is. While absolutely secure in his masculinity, he will cry, even in public.

He's also so very supportive of any of my endeavours. I'd never have written/published my books if it weren't for his 'go for it'.

I know Leos who are excellent at making people feel a warm, fuzzy glow of happiness just by being in their presence. It's as if they are radiating some concealed energy that we love to have. They also won't hold back in telling you, or demonstrating to you how much they like or love you. You can guarantee that the person you know who has arranged a surprise birthday party, or made a collection for a charity, or written 'I Love You' in the sky with a jet contrail is probably a Leo.

Dramatic

I always thought I should be treated like a star.
Madonna

My dictionary defines 'dramatic' as *'of drama, sudden and exciting or unexpected, vividly striking.'* I think this quite sums up part of the Leo character.

The drama that a Leo enjoys can be literal, as in enjoying

being on radio or TV, or figuratively in being a 'drama-king/queen' and wanting everything and everyone to revolve around them.

Here is Isabella describing her son Harry when he was small:

There is something about drama here. Harry was a dramatic little boy and he wanted to be noticed. He was never ever shy and was very confident with adults. He loved parties, especially ones where he got a lot of attention. When he was about three we were out for the day and we had tea in a village hall with a stage. Harry got on to the stage and started dancing about so that everybody could see him. It was very funny and he made everybody laugh. In fact it was hard to get him off the stage when we were leaving...

As Leo is a Fire sign, they're swifter to react to things and also quicker to take offence. They prefer an appreciate audience, no matter how small that might be. This isn't meant in a negative way. They genuinely can like or enjoy all eyes on them. I know a Leo Dad that sadly died of cancer. Even on his deathbed, he enjoyed a quartet of musicians serenading him in the hospital where he was a patient. Compare this to a Virgo, who would more likely curl up inside if you so much raised your voice in a hospital ward, let alone had four young ladies playing violin, viola, cello and flute.

On the literal side of drama, there are endless amounts of Leo actors, singers, dancers and creatives, who like to bring their talents to amuse and entertain.

When I asked my Leo volunteers how they'd prefer to be lavished, not one of them suggested a quiet, domestic scenario:

Helping people, particularly in creative ways – I am currently volunteering for my local Arts Centre and totally love it! I also love walking my dog, walking in nature and doing anything creative. Just did the Race for Life and that made me very happy – both the fundraising and the taking part. I would like to be surprised by a trip to somewhere in the country or by the sea to have a lovely day out with great food and not have to worry about money.

Optimistic

I don't think I've ever met a truly sad Leo. I've seen depressed Leos but that's not the same as gloomy or sad. That's not to say that they don't exist, but, as yet, they haven't made an appointment to see me. The Leos I have seen, even if they're in a really bad way, will want to talk things through, and go away feeling that what they're going to do, or have done, is validated.

Unlike an Air sign, I don't have to come up with billions of ideas to help them along. No, they just want to know that what they're doing is 'right'. Which can be a little subjective. Like all fixed signs, Leo doesn't like change, and as long as what they're planning or involved in is legal and decent, I'm not going to argue.

Their optimism mostly centres around their outlook on life, which is generally positive.

Alan is a Leo Homeopath and author who lives and works in the USA. He also edits an online Homeopathy newsletter and makes funny little homeopathy cartoons to keep us all smiling. Here are his views on optimism:

For me, optimism is not the idea that fortune always smiles on us, but the belief that problems can be solved and crises endured, as long as we stay present, keep our courage and be open to all the possibilities. It helps to understand that good fortune and bad fortune are deeply connected, and one always leads to the other.

They view life as a playful place, with lots of fun things going on, with everyone getting along and helping each other out. When I was a child, a popular author was Leo Enid Blyton. She only wrote children's books and created Noddy and the Famous Five series with motivating titles like *Five on a Treasure Island* and *Five Have a Mystery to Solve.*

In one of her books she has a character say:

The best way to treat obstacles is to use them as stepping stones. Laugh at them, tread on them, and let them lead you to something better.

Which could almost be a call sign for Leo.

Vain

My dictionary defines vanity as: 'conceit and desire for admiration because of one's personal attainments or attractions.'

The downside to the Leo character is a tendency for un-evolved Leos to be self-obsessed. They can think that the whole world revolves around them, which isn't entirely true, as we know that the Earth revolves around the Sun…

I remember a song from my teen years called *You're So Vain* by Carly Simon (who is Sun sign Cancer) which had the catch-line, 'you probably think this song is about you,' and that nicely sums up the sort of problems we can encounter when the Leo ego gets too big.

They can construct, in their mind, that they are the most important person in their family, their city, their country… and if you're really unlucky, the world. This self-inflated issue only arises because of a deep need to feel acknowledged and admired by others.

There are Leos who are aware of this vanity. Leo Poet Laureate Ted Hughes wrote a poem called "The Decay of Vanity":

Now it is seven years since you were the Queen That crowned me King: and six years since your ghost Left your body cold in my arms as a stone…[10]

I loved the way the poem has a King, a Queen and Vanity all in it, and it is written by a Leo!

There are some lovely Leo quotes attributed to Napoleon Bonaparte:

I am sometimes a fox and sometimes a lion. The whole secret of government lies in knowing when to be the one or the other.

And

The herd seek out the great, not for their sake but for their influence; and the great welcome them out of vanity or need.

Makes you wonder if Napoleon's welcome was for vanity or need!

Childish vs. Childlike

Leo has a wonderfully childlike view of the world. They see it in rays of shining light and love to go 'wow' at things. They enjoy the company of their admirers, to be the centre of attention, to feel as if everyone is a friend.

This child-like view can sometime swing into being child-ish, which is a completely different story.

I once worked with a Leo lady. Her father was an alcoholic, and she and he lived the most awful life. She still hadn't left home, even though she was in her late 30s and she told me (constantly) that she wanted to get married and have children of her own, except she just couldn't grow up.

To 'grow up' she would have to leave home, but her father was convinced she had a personality disorder, when in fact his drinking must have clouded any judgement he could make.

He was an ex-psychiatrist, and was violent and verbally abusive. This poor woman would tell me about how unreasonable her father was, and how he told her what to do... but their relationship seemed to be codependent and impossible to fathom.

Eventually she got her own flat, but her father still berated her and badgered her and kept telling her how useless and ill she was and how no one would ever want her. He kept saying how she needed treatment; she kept saying how overbearing he was.

Her parents were divorced, acrimoniously.

This lady really had a difficulty with what's involved in growing up. From her view everything that adults did brought sadness and unhappiness, so by continuing to live with her father, she could stay his baby and be loved and cared for. Except there was no caring at all, just lots of anger and misunderstanding.

It was only when her mother died that she managed to see how being with her father (who was a Gemini) had held her back from her dreams and one day she just disappeared from town and I never saw her again. I hope she managed to make a life for herself.

Cats and Pets

I once knew another Leo lady who kept *very* expensive Persian cats. She worried about them constantly. Her children had all left home and the cats were almost substitute babies. I visited her house and she'd put the cats safely in another room as they were a little shy and the party was a bit noisy. She let me peek into the room where they were and I must say it was the weirdest thing I've ever seen. There were the five cats. Each one was sitting on what looked like a little throne. They were immaculately groomed and each one was wearing a little collar with pretty bows. They looked as contented and well cared for as a cat can look and they had a sort of 'worship me' air about them. Their little noses almost seemed to be turned-up at me as if saying, *'I hope you realise how wonderful I am.'*

Leo Percy Bysshe Shelley had a funny relationship with his

cats and wrote:

When my cats aren't happy, I'm not happy. Not because I care about their mood but because I know they're just sitting there thinking up ways to get even.

Some Leo writers like George Bernard Shaw have even stronger views:

Animals are my friends... and I don't eat my friends.

However, not *all* Leos like cats. JK Rowling is allergic but quite a lot of Leos love to have animals as pets.

Chapter Two

How to Make a Chart

Making a Birth Chart is much easier these days. Before the invention of computers, which wasn't so long ago, you'd have to get a thing called an Ephemeris, which listed all the planets in their signs, then plot where the place of birth was, with longitude and latitude, and taking into account random things like 'local time' and 'war time' and that terribly annoying thing 'summer time' and put this here, and place that there. I couldn't even think about making a chart until it was easy. And now it's easy-peasy.

All you need to know are three pieces of personal information, to get three Astrological pieces of information:

The date of birth, the time of birth and the location of birth.

This will give you the Sun sign, Ascendant (or rising sign) and Moon sign of the person you are making the chart for.

So where will we get that Astrological information? And will it cost you anything?

The answer is on the Internet and (at the moment) it's free.

The website we're going to use is a wonderful one based in Switzerland, overlooking Lake Zurich and the company is called Astrodienst, which means Astro Service in German.

The website address is www.astro.com which is also nice and easy to remember. There are a number of other websites that will give you a chart for free, but the reason we're using this one is because it's reliable. Some things are free, but they're certainly not accurate, reliable or useful.

Go to the site and make an account.

When you're all set up, go back to the website and find the page called Free Horoscopes.

On that page, scroll to the bottom of the page and find the page called Extended Chart Selection.

This is the page that will let you make a chart using a different system from the default system which is called Placidus. This was invented by a chappie called Placidus and makes the segments in the chart, which we call the houses, unequal, and also is a more modern method and one almost every website and computer programme uses. I prefer the more ancient system called Equal House, which as the name suggests makes the houses (segments) of the chart into equal sizes.

You are now on the Extended Chart Selection page.

There are lots of boxes, with lots of things written in them. Don't worry; ignore all of them except the one that says House System.

In the box it will say 'default', we need to change that to say 'equal'.

Now click the button that says 'show the chart' and on the next page that comes up, will be your chart.

That's all you need to do.

There will be lots of lines going from planet to planet, ignore them too. We only need three pieces of information.

The **sign** of the **Ascendant,** the **sign** of the **Moon** and the location/**house** that the **Sun** is in.

The houses are numbered 1–12 in an anticlockwise order.

These are the shapes representing the signs, so find the one that matches yours. They are called glyphs.

Aries ♈

Taurus ♉

Gemini ♊

Cancer ♋

Leo ♌

Virgo ♍

Libra ♎

Scorpio ♏

Sagittarius ♐

Capricorn ♑

Aquarius ♒

Pisces ♓

This is the symbol for the Sun ☉

This is the symbol for the Moon ☽

The Elements

To understand your Leo fully, you must take into account which Element their Ascendant and Moon are in.

Each sign of the Zodiac has been given an element that it operates under: Earth, Air, Fire and Water. I like to think of them as operating at different 'speeds'.

The **Earth** signs are **Taurus, Virgo** and **Capricorn**. The Earth Element is stable, grounded and concerned with practical matters. A Leo with a lot of Earth in their chart works best at a very slow, steady speed. (I refer to these in the text as 'Earthy'.)

The **Air** signs are **Gemini, Libra** and **Aquarius** (who is the 'Water-carrier' *not* a Water sign). The Air element enjoys ideas, concepts and thoughts. It operates at a faster speed than Earth, not as fast as Fire but faster than Water and Earth. Imagine them as being medium speed. (I refer to these as 'Air 'signs.)

The **Fire** signs are **Aries**, our friend **Leo** and **Sagittarius**. The Fire element likes action, excitement and can be very impatient. Their speed is *very* fast. (I refer to these as 'Firey' i.e. Fire Sign.)

The **Water** signs are **Cancer, Scorpio** and **Pisces**. The Water element involves feelings, impressions, hunches and intuition. They operate faster than Earth but not as fast as Air. A sort of slow-medium speed. (I refer to these as 'Water' signs.)

Chapter Three

The Ascendant

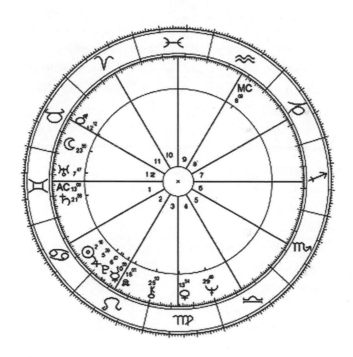

Name: ♂ Mick Jagger
born on Mo., 26 July 1943
in Dartford, ENG (UK)
0e14, 51n27

Time: 2:30 am
Univ.Time: 0:30
Sid. Time: 20:42:17

For our example chart, we're going to use the birth data for Mick Jagger, the lead singer of the Rolling Stones. Most people have heard of him and we know his birth time and place so his chart will be accurate.

Mick was born on 26th July 1943, at 2.30am in the morning in Dartford, England.

If you input all that data, you should end up with a chart looking like the one above. Your chart will have a lot of lines from planet to planet but I've taken them out as it makes the chart look a little busy. Just ignore them, as we don't need to take them in account for this purpose.

If you look closely at the chart above, you'll see the initials AC at the quarter to nine position.

This is astrological shorthand for Ascendant. In Mick's chart, his Ascendant is in the sign of Gemini. Round the outside of the circle are all the signs of the Zodiac, which we learned about in the last chapter, so skip back there and check them out.

This is the symbol for Gemini Ⅱ and as you'll see in Mick's chart, the AC initials are located in the middle of that sign.

Now, we know Mick is a Leo as he was born on the 26th July but because he was born very early in the morning the sign that was rising over the eastern horizon at 2.30am where he was born was Gemini. If he'd been born at 4am… it'd be Cancer and if he'd been born at 6am… it would be Leo, so this is why the *time* of birth is important.

We consider the Ascendant in astrology as being the most important part of a chart, and if you don't know the time of birth, this won't apply, so skip this chapter.

The Ascendant is like the glasses you wear, the face you show people on first meeting, the bit of you that comes out when you're under stress or put on the spot. Most people will never know what Sun sign you are. If they only know you casually, all they will 'see' and experience is your rising sign or Ascendant.

As it is defined by your actual moment of birth, it is the 'way' you came into the world. Maybe if your Ascendant is Taurus, you took your time being born, and came into the world slowly and deliberately. Maybe if your Ascendant is Aries you came into the world full of energy and screaming!

This isn't 'who' you are, just your mode of life experience.

A Leo with an Aries ascendant is going to be more active, energetic and possibly even more aggressive than a Leo with a Pisces Ascendant, who might be 'softer' and more emotional.

Mick is still a Leo, no doubt about that, but his Ascendant is in

Gemini, giving him the 'gift of the gab' and capable of talking/chatting and being conversational even in other languages! He's bilingual. I saw a YouTube video of him speaking very well in French during a short interview and he was happily listening to and answering the questions in French.

So I've put together all the various Ascendants or rising signs your Leo might have, and each example has a little quote from the Leo that we know has that Ascendant.

Aries Ascendant

Musicians don't retire; they stop when there's no more music in them.
Louis Armstrong

As the first sign of the Zodiac and represented by the Ram, Aries Ascendant is fearless and brave, most of the time. They enjoy moving forwards swiftly, having action orientated solutions and makes for a speedy combination for a Leo. They're unlikely to sit around waiting for things to happen. More likely to be the instigator and initiator.

Taurus Ascendant

Anything worth doing is worth doing slowly.
Mae West

Represented by the Bull, Taurus Ascendant for a Leo brings a more steady approach to life. They enjoy taking their time, indulging the senses and take a practical sensory viewpoint. If they don't want to do something, they certainly won't be persuaded by any means.

Gemini Ascendant

A lot of times songs are very much of a moment, that you just encapsulate. They come to you, you write them, you feel good that

day, or bad that day.
Mick Jagger

Gemini 'the Twins' loves conversation and being able to chat, in any language to anyone. They might be bi- or multi-lingual, good at conversation and love to debate the night away. Their mobile phone is always at the ready and a Leo with this Ascendant will enjoy chatting to all and sundry.

Cancer Ascendant

People don't try to show their feelings, they try to hide them.
Robert De Niro

As the more feeling sign of the Zodiac, Cancer Ascendant gives a Leo a more family orientated approach. They will see their life through rosy, homey glasses and will want snuggles and cuddles and puppies all around.

Leo Ascendant

Everyone will be famous for 15 minutes.
Andy Warhol

A Leo with a Leo Ascendant just cannot be ignored. You will see them coming from 50 paces. They are confident, looking at the world through optimistic glasses and get others as excited as they are about what they're doing. This Asc makes for an extra helping of Leo qualities.

Virgo Ascendant

The twins are very good travellers. Of course we'd never put their health at risk for anything, because that's what's most important.
Roger Federer

This can be rather a tricky Asc for a Leo to have. There is their Asc wanting things to be calculated, exact, on-time and perfect. There's their Sun sign wanting to get things done ASAP with no thought of the consequences. The upshot is someone who is more cautious, more careful and more capable of being health aware and precise. A definite juggling act.

Libra Ascendant

Flirtation begins innocently but could become hot and heavy.
Sydney Omarr

Libra is the sign of relationships and especially the romantic ones. They want to cover the world with love and have everyone being peaceful and happy. They prefer others to be polite and gracious, with no small amount of taste and niceness. Matching and complementary surroundings make them feel settled and content.

Scorpio Ascendant

I have always wanted a solo career, deep in the darkest pit of myself, but I didn't dare admit it to myself even. It took me a long time to confront my fears.
Geri Halliwell

This is the Asc that takes risks and penetrates those deep dark places that others would gladly shy away from. A Leo with Scorpio Asc will not stand for any nonsense, and loves to push the boundaries of transformation by being focused and intense. They love to feel they are in control.

Sagittarius Ascendant

Oh, I'm a big-mouth. I said a lot of things.
Sean Penn

As Sagittarius is ruled by benevolent Jupiter the God-of-making-things-bigger, you can guarantee a Leo with this Asc will be firing their arrows of exaggeration directly at you. As another Fire sign, they'll be active, energetic and full of their own sense of self. They'll have a philosophical view of life and enjoy the funness of travel and other cultures.

Capricorn Ascendant

In life, all good things come hard, but wisdom is the hardest to come by.
Lucille Ball

Capricorn is ruled by stern Saturn, the God of Hard Knocks, so a Leo with this Asc will have a more realistic outlook on life. They will be aware of the hard work necessary to gain their dreams and to be practical and truthful. Even if it means pointing out things you might not want to hear.

Aquarius Ascendant

If you're looking for the safe choice, you shouldn't be supporting a black guy named Barack Obama to be the next leader of the free world.
Barack Obama

This is the sign that loves freedom more than anything. You can't restrain their independence or love of friendship and humanity. They adore computers and technical equipment and anything with a label 'new' on it.

Pisces Ascendant

When all of my dreams are a heartbeat away and the answers are all up to me. Give me one moment in time.
Whitney Houston

As Pisces is the sign of extra emotions and intuition, it doesn't sit happily with the Leo Sun and can make for someone who feels confused and unsure a lot of the time. On a good day those extrasensory abilities assist them in tuning into their life purpose. On a bad day they just can't wake up to the real world and prefer to escape.

Chapter Four

The Moon

If the Sun in Astrology represents our 'ego' or 'who' we are, then the Moon, just like it does in real life, reflects the light back from the Sun and represents our feelings or our inner self. The part of us we don't always show until we're feeling emotional.

You could say that the Sun is male and the Moon is female, but those distinctions aren't so relevant today. They're more likely to symbolise our active self and our passive self.

I'm not suggesting that we have multiple personalities; what I am suggesting is we have a conscious and a subconscious bit.

In our chart example, Mick has his Moon in the sign of Taurus, so even though he's a Leo with all that brash, in-your-face energy, emotionally he's a bit of a lover of good food and sensuousness. Which if you read some old write-ups about his former years, with all the drug taking and wild partying, sort of makes sense.

The astrological Moon therefore is how we react to things that have an emotional component. And it's a good idea to find out your own Moon sign, and that of the Leos you know.

Once you get an understanding of your Moon and your Sun signs, you're almost on the way to deep acceptance of yourself. Imagine. There you are, a sensitive Cancer Sun sign, and you've got Moon in active, go-getting Sagittarius... and you can't work out why you want to travel all the time when your write-up in the newspaper says you're a home bird.

I could never understand the description of my Pisces sign, until I found out I've got Moon in chatty Gemini. It just didn't make sense that I should be so chatty and talkative. Now I know why!

So, find out your Leo's Moon sign, and you'll be well on the way to true knowledge.

The Dr Bach Flower Essences

In 1933 Dr Edward Bach, a medical doctor and Homeopath, published a little booklet called *The Twelve Healers and Other Remedies*. His theory was that if the emotional component a person was suffering from was removed, their 'illness' would also disappear. I tend to agree with this kind of thinking as most illnesses (except being hit by a bus) are preceded by an unhappy event or an emotional disruption that then sets into place the body getting out of sync. Removing the emotional issue and bringing a bit of stability into someone's life, when they are having a hard time, can improve their overall health so much that wellness resumes.

Knowing which Bach Flower Essence can help certain worries and upsetments gives you and your Leo more control over your lives. I recommend the essences a lot in my practice if I feel a certain part of a person's chart is under stress... and usually it's the Moon that needs help. The essences describe the negative aspects of the character, which are focused on during treatment. This awareness helps reverse those trends, so when our emotional selves are nice and comfortable we can then face each day with more strength.

I've quoted Dr Bach's actual words for each sign.

To use the Essences take 2 drops from the stock bottle and put it into a glass of water and sip. I tend to recommend putting them into a small water bottle, and sipping them throughout the day, at least 4 times. For young children, do the same.

Remember to seek medical attention if symptoms don't get better and/or seek professional counselling.

So here are the various Moon signs your Leo might have, and again I've included little quotes from each person to illustrate how their Moon is expressed with the Leo Sun.

Aries Moon

If you haven't turned rebel by twenty you've got no heart.
Kevin Spacey

This is the Moon that is quick to get all worked-up about things, and like a Summer storm, it soon passes and they're back to their 'normal' self. They're active and energetic emotionally and totally honest about how they feel. The Ram pushes hard though to get what it wants, so if you're opposing them, you're in for a fight.
Bach Flower Essence Impatiens:

Those who are quick in thought and action and who wish all things to be done without hesitation or delay.

Taurus Moon

I never resist temptation, because I have found that things that are bad for me do not tempt me.
George Bernard Shaw

This Moon loves all things sensual and sexy. Chocolate, good wine, silk sheets, anything where the senses are pandered and satisfied. Taurus the Bull loves things to be constant and unchanging, so routine is important as is meals-on-time.
Bach Flower Essence Gentian:

Those who are easily discouraged. They may be progressing well in the affairs of their daily life, but any small delay or hindrance to progress causes doubt and soon disheartens them.

Gemini Moon

Guard your roving thoughts with a jealous care, for speech is but the dialer of thoughts, and every fool can plainly read in your words what is the hour of your thoughts.
Alfred Lord Tennyson

As the eternal child, Gemini never wants to grow old! This is the Moon sign of two options and opinions as they are the astrological twins. They like discussion, argument, conversation and for things to be (as this is an Air sign) cerebral and interesting. Short journeys are loved too.

Bach Flower Essence Cerato:

Those who have not sufficient confidence in themselves to make their own decisions.

Cancer Moon

Dreams have encircled me, I said, From careless childhood's sunny time; Visions by ardent fancy fed, Since life was in its morning prime.

Emily Brontë

The Cancer Moon is happiest when they can be aware of their emotions, feel safe, nurtured, cuddled and snuggled. As Cancer is 'ruled' by the Moon it's in its home sign. They can be cranky and moody but equally they will love deeply. They will also love Mum/Mom, the home and all things aged and traditional.

Bach Flower Essence Clematis:

Living in the hopes of happier times, when their ideals may come true.

Leo Moon

I am not the President. Instead, I hold an even higher office, that of citizen of the United States.

Martin Sheen

This is a cheery, optimistic Moon but ignore it at your peril! They love to bask in the glow of the love from their entourage, enjoy the red-carpet treatment, wince if you forget their name and love you if you thank them profusely for their kindness, which will be great.

Bach Flower Essence Vervain:

Those with fixed principles and ideas, which they are confident are right.

Virgo Moon

Health food may be good for the conscience but Oreos taste a hell of a lot better.

Robert Redford

As Virgo is the sign of health and healing and analysis, on a good day their powers of classification are a joy and they have an enormous memory for irrelevant information. They will happily dot every 'i' and cross every 't' and remind you that you said this and that on certain dates.

Bach Flower Essence Centaury:

Their good nature leads them to do more than their own share of work and they may neglect their own mission in life.

Libra Moon

What a man does for pay is of little significance. What he is, as a sensitive instrument responsive to the world's beauty, is everything!

HP Lovecraft

This is the classic sign of indecision represented by the balancing scales that form the sign of Libra. Should I do this? Or that? Or something else? Their concerns will centre around close personal relationships and they are at their happiest with a ring on their finger and someone to love. Fairness and balance are also important.

Bach Flower Essence Scleranthus:

Those who suffer from being unable to decide between two things, first one seeming right then the other.

Scorpio Moon

The screen is a magic medium. It has such power that it can retain interest as it conveys emotions and moods that no other art form can hope to tackle.
Stanley Kubrick

If you think of the colour deep, deep red you'll get an idea of what it's like to have a Scorpio Moon. Deep feelings, deep thoughts and even deep resentments if they're frustrated in their desires. There are no half-measures. All, or nothing. They will stick through thick and thin if they're on your side. They will stop at nothing if you're not.
Bach Flower Essence Chicory:

They are continually correcting what they consider wrong and enjoy doing so.

Sagittarius Moon

The one thing I regret was that my work required an enormous amount of my time, and a lot of travel.
Neil Armstrong

As a Fire sign and one of the more swift-speed Moons, Sagittarius Moon wants to answer all of life's questions, or at least ask them and investigate. Any sort of learning or teaching will keep them amused as will contact with foreign countries and other civilisations. On the downside, they love to 'be right' so be careful not to challenge their beliefs too much.

This Essence comes under the heading 'Over-Sensitive to Influences and Ideas'.
Bach Flower Essence Agrimony:

They hide their cares behind their humour and jesting and try to bear their trials with cheerfulness.

Capricorn Moon

When you go through hardships and decide not to surrender, that is strength.
Arnold Schwarzenegger

Capricorn is ruled by strict Saturn, the planet of 'hard-knocks'. They will learn at an early age that life isn't always fluffy and fun. They prefer serious subjects, sensible ideas and life built on firm foundations. They will also put up with more than any other sign and be stoic in how they tackle life's challenges.
Bach Flower Essence Mimulus:

Fear of worldly things, illness, pain, accident, poverty, of the dark, of being alone, of misfortune. They secretly bear their dread and do not speak freely of it to others.

Aquarius Moon

I had friends but I was spending a great deal of my time alone and for me that was vital because there's an awful lot you learn about yourself when you're alone.
Kate Bush

Friendship with a capital 'F' rules Aquarius. Ruled by wacky Uranus this allows weird and wonderful ideas and friendships to be born. Full of ideas and crazy thoughts they will draw you into their world view, which is inclusive and utopian. Whether or not they are happy as a human being is debatable.
Bach Flower Essence Water Violet:

For those who like to be alone, very independent, capable and self-reliant. They are aloof and go their own way.

Pisces Moon

How can you consider flower power outdated? The essence of my lyrics is the desire for peace and harmony. That's all anyone has ever wanted. How could it become outdated?
Robert Plant

As the last sign of the Zodiac and one that is supremely sensitive to fairies, angels, and all things spiritual and other-worldly, a Leo with Moon in Pisces can act like the martyr. Feeling life's ills and upsetments deeply. On a bad day, they sense all the suffering in the world, which will make them feel weak and low. Just make sure you guide them back to earth occasionally...
Bach Flower Essence Rock Rose:

For cases where there even appears no hope or when the person is very frightened or terrified.

Chapter Five

The Houses

Now we know two major things about our friend the Leo. One, what his/her Sun sign is all about, and two, what sign his/her Moon is in.

To make this understanding even more astrological we're going to learn which house their Sun falls into.

If you look back at Mick's chart on page 21 you will see that the symbol for the Sun is located in the section of the chart marked 2.

Look back at the picture of his chart and you will see that the circle has been divided into 12 equal portions. Bit like a pizza.

Each portion of the circle is called a 'house'. They used to be called 'mansions' because they contained and were 'home' to the location of the Sun.

If you were born just as the Sun was coming up over the horizon, your Sun would be located in the first part of the chart in the first house. The later in the day you're born, the further round the circle your Sun would land.

This is because the Sun rises in the east and sets in the west and the birth chart is a little map of the location, on the day when you were born.

Obviously, there are plenty of other planets that were in the sky on your birthday, but all we need to concern ourselves with is where the Sun was located in the chart you are making for your Leo friend/lover/relative.

Now, there is a big difference astrologically between someone with their Sun in the 3rd house to someone with their Sun in the 7th.

The meanings of the house locations are not something that can be proved I'm afraid, so you'll just have to take my word for it. But the original thinking behind it was: *Here's the map I've made* *of Mr/Ms Leo, there **must** be a difference to him/her being born at 8am to him/her being born at 6pm.*

How to Read Your Astrological Chart by Donna Cunningham (a wonderful book all students in astrology should read) says:

If the intermediate cusps were real divisions rather than artificial ones, there wouldn't be such a controversy about them.[11]

Quite right. There is no obvious reason why each house means something until you start comparing people's charts and immersing yourself in the subject.

I appreciate it's a big leap of faith for non-astrologers to understand the whole house thing, and if you don't have an accurate time of birth, please skip this chapter.

If you do have a correct birth time, then carry on reading.

I have listed the houses in order, with their meaning, and again I've given real-life examples and quotes of people with those configurations.

If you'd like more information on the houses, there is a section on the astro.com website.

Here are the different interpretations for the different houses that the Sun could fall into in your Leo's chart. The first house represents the beginning of daylight, the dawn of the day and the houses go round anticlockwise.

In your Leo's chart, their Sun could be in any of the houses, so check where it's located and read the interpretation for that house placement.

The First House, House of Personality

An apology? Bah! Disgusting! Cowardly! Beneath the dignity of any gentleman, however wrong he might be.
Steve Martin

With the Leo Sun here, the native is forceful, energetic and

37

active. They are confident and not afraid of Mr Wolf. They prefer to lead rather than follow and enjoy a faster pace of life.

The Second House, House of Money, Material Possessions and Self-Worth

Lack of money is the root of all evil.
George Bernard Shaw

This is the house that represents the things that a person owns. The practical world. Energy will be spent on accumulating possessions or financial security. Enjoyment will be found from holding, touching, truly experiencing things… tactile experiences like massage are generally treasured.

The Third House, House of Communication & Short Journeys

I have this strange habit of having language come out of my mouth as a result of thought.
Shelley Winters

Like the third sign Gemini, the third house wants to engage with others by communicating with them. They would need a mobile phone, access to letters, telephones, conversations and all forms of communication. Being able to chat or write satisfies this house. As it also governs short journeys, having some means of local transport is good.

The Fourth House, House of Home, Family & Roots

I've been pondering how we belong to others, to our parents, children, other relatives, friends, co-workers, neighbours, ancestors.
Amy Shapiro

This is where the home becomes important. 'Family' in all its varied combinations will be a high priority. Cooking, snuggling up to others, pets, being close to significant others and the domestic world are all important.

The Fifth House, House of Creativity & Romance

My children are not royal; they just happen to have the Queen for their aunt.
Princess Margaret

The fifth house is concerned with being able to shine. Being the centre of attention is also a plus. Red carpets, heaps of praise and appreciative recognition keeps the Sun in this house happy. Being artistic and creative, or giving birth to children or writing are all expressed here.

The Sixth House, House of Work & Health

A sex symbol is a heavy load to carry when one is tired, hurt, and bewildered.
Clara Bow

The sixth house has its focus on everything related to health. It also is the work that we do. The Leo Sun here will want to be well, healthy and organised. It's also not unheard of for them to work in the health and healing sector or, at the very least, to be concerned with their own and others' health.

The Seventh House, House of Relationships & Marriage

I just liked the idea of being engaged.
Belinda Carlisle

The Leo Sun here will want to share their life with another significant other. Being single won't wash. Until their close personal relationship is organised life feels bleak. When attached, life has new meaning.

The Eighth House, House of Life Force in Birth, Sex, Death & Afterlife

I'm not funny. What I am is brave.
Lucille Ball

The intensity of the eighth house with the Leo Sun makes an individual who is strong in character and un-swayed from their life's mission. Boredom is not on the menu! The ability to focus exclusively on one thing at a time can bring great results.

The Ninth House, House of Philosophy & Long Distance Travel

I travelled extensively through Europe, North Africa and overland to India. During this period I began drawing and painting mandalas and developed an interest in Astrology.
AT Mann

Provided that the ninth house Sun in Leo can philosophise about life's true meaning all is well. Foreign countries, long journeys, and an interest in other cultures will be expressed here. Keep passports at the ready.

The Tenth House, House of Social Identity & Career

Ambition never is in a greater hurry than I; it merely keeps pace with circumstances and with my general way of thinking.
Napoleon Bonaparte

You would expect the tenth house individual to be focused on their career and how they feel others perceive them. Being able to be recognised in their chosen field no matter how long this may take will guide them to success.

The Eleventh House, House of Social Life & Friendships

Because primarily of the power of the Internet, people of modest means can band together and amass vast sums of money that can change the world for some public good if they all agree.
Bill Clinton

The Leo Sun in the eleventh house individual will want, no *need*: friends, groups, organisations, affiliations and/or societies that they can/will be members of. They don't see themselves in isolation to the world, they are part of it. Friendships are top of the list, so is charitable work and uniting the planet.

The Twelfth House, House of Spirituality

That was a tough stretch with a lot of emotions – getting married, expecting the births, was all energy-consuming. On top of that I had so much success, so it was a lot of things at once. But I feel like I'm refreshed again. That's great. Spending some time with the babies in a completely private way was key.
Roger Federer

I have noticed a lot of my clients who have Sun in the twelfth really don't like living in the 'real world'. It all seems too painful and insensitive. The twelfth house, like the sign Pisces, wants to merge with the fairies and angels and escape to Never Never Land. They feel better where they have somewhere to escape to emotionally be that the beach, on a hilltop, or in a nice warm bath every now and then.

Chapter Six

The Difficulties

So far I've been painting quite a rosy picture of our friend the Leo. However, like everything in life, there is always some room for upsetments, disappointments and misunderstandings.

My job involves helping clients move on and deal with life's unhappy events (I call them upsetments) and I will see in private practice a big mix of different problems.

What I will be demonstrating here is the sort of difficulties that your average Leo will fall victim to, or what the average client will complain about the Leo in their life.

Obviously, there is no such thing as an average client, but I'm sure you understand what I mean.

Here are the details of a young man called William. He has an Aquarius Ascendant, Moon also in Aquarius and Sun in the 7th house. His Sagittarius mother Sophie gave me some information about him.

Loyal and affectionate within the family, though sometimes prickly. Popular with friends, girls and within the music bands he helped form.

At school, an August birthday meant the permanent debate – a younger or an older group? He much preferred the latter and regrets that he was put in the younger group. He missed his friends. During the A level years at Further Education College he was not consistent with his studying and the wise Head suggested he take a year off to work. He was pleased to do this, and successfully managed one of the new kitchen shops before successfully resuming his A levels at college.

Not very sporty, joined modern dance group at Uni. Good swimmer, but put off by the need to protect his ears with ear plugs.

In recent years has done much sailing and walking.

A multi-talented person, despite the deafness, was musical from an early age, played classical and electric guitar by ear and by music. Writes very well, degree in English and History of Art. Journalism school, then a reporter's job. Travel, bar jobs, then a job on a new channel's breakfast show, while gigging in spare time. Eventually he went off to USA, West Coast hoping to make it to the top in music. I think the choice of Santa Barbara (small, Spanish) rather than LA suits him well and says much about him.

Always makes where he lives attractive, favours good design and craftsmanship. Aged 16 painted his bedroom ceiling gloss red. Dresses in stylish, casual clothes as good quality as he can afford.

He is very informed about health, environmental and food pollution. In recent years he has been diagnosed as possibly ADHD and for years his health has been highly absorbing for him. He could be described as a pacific anarchist, he mistrusts authority but would do no harm, unlikely to protest, even peacefully.

After several longish relationships he is very happily committed to a colleague 20+ years his junior who feels the same. They will marry next May, a family wedding. He is very affectionate, excellent with his little nephews and if they have children, he will be a very caring father.

As Mum is also a Fire sign, there is no lack of love, affection and action in the relationship. What she finds difficult is his Aquarius Ascendant and Moon as they can indicate a more self-sufficient emotional attitude.

The piece about him missing his friends would be an alarm bell for me, as friends are supremely important to someone with Aquarius planets.

He also has all his planets on one side of the circle, making his chart a bowl shape but I don't have space in this book to go into that; however, there is lots of information on my website www.maryenglish.com/indigo1.htm about Indigo birth charts.

Another mother I spoke to is Nadine, who is a full-time Mum and witch. She has two children, one of which is a Leo daughter. Here are her views on this sign:

Leos are faithful, adoring and jolly, but can become fixated if there is a problem they cannot solve and never walk away in an argument – they need the final word!

So what sort of things might upset your Leo (or upset you) so much that you consider it a problem? Here are the types of things I come across in my private practice and that I've noticed about some (not all) Leos.

My Leo wants to buy a big house in the country/town/city and spend lots of money decorating/altering it.

This is something that you will have to watch. The optimistic Leo outlook on life, especially financially, will ignore the minor details of not being able to afford something and will aim high towards their dream. The problem with this is they will eventually become tangled and hard-to-live-with when the banks foreclose on the deal or they wake up one day with massive debts.

Don't get taken in by the optimism.

Mere optimism does NOT pay the bills! And knowing Leo's taste for luxury and drama, they can be high.

If you're a Taurus or a Capricorn, you'll already be quaking in your boots thinking about the 'waste' of money or the expenditure, while more busy signs won't notice there is a problem until their card doesn't work when they go shopping.

The ideal solution is to be completely honest, and demonstrate to your Leo that as much as you may love them, you don't want to get into debt; and if they want to go wild with credit cards, they'd better get their own job and cards, and you're not responsible for the outcome.

When it comes to house decorating, I often wonder if the people that have lions on their house-gates, or some other sort of showy statues on display are Leos, or at least have Leo Ascendant or Moon...

My Leo doesn't like my sister, brother, mother, other relative, close friend(s), significant other, spouse and won't be polite about it.

I'm afraid a Leo isn't a Libra. Their levels of tact and diplomacy are not in good supply if they don't like someone. They could come out with catty comments, or make rude remarks at the wrong time in the wrong place. The best way to deal with this is to just accept the situation and try and avoid too many family clashes. You certainly can't make any fixed-sign (Taurus, Leo, Scorpio or Aquarius) change their mind about something they feel strongly about, so don't waste your energy trying.

If you can think of something good about the relationship, anything, you can focus on that rather than the difficulty. You might find your Leo doesn't like your relative because they feel slighted or ignored in some way. This really doesn't go down well with a Leo.

However, as much as you can want things to go a certain way, don't make a big issue of it, as it will only cause what Leos love, which is a drama... and that could go on for years and years.

It would be better to *ask* your Leo, not *tell* him/her, to be civil to that person because s/he is important to you, and you would really appreciate it if they would do you that small favour. Your Leo does not need to be close to the person, but just to endure. Leos cannot resist pleadings and sacrifice – they are knights-errant after all.

Be sure to show your appreciation and give thanks and lots of praise afterwards (good cooking, gifts or pampering will do).

My Leo doesn't seem to care about *my* feelings.

This does happen. Even though Leo is one of the more caring signs, they won't notice you're upset if you're not dramatically throwing yourself around the house, weeping and sighing. Your Leo cares a lot about your feelings, but if you're the quiet sort, or a Water or Earth sign and given to being stoic and holding back your feelings, how ever is your Leo going to know you're upset?

It might take one enormous argument or shouting match, with doors slamming and lots of raised voices, for your Leo to get the picture.

I knew a Pisces lady who was dating a Leo. I wrote about her in my *How to Survive a Pisces*. Her Leo had Moon in Scorpio, so was very passionate but all that drama began to wear her down.

You will have to accept your Leo exactly as they are and not try to change them. John Gray talks at length in his *Venus and Mars on a Date* about how women newly into a relationship become members of the 'Home Improvement Committee' and try and change their man into something else. If you don't like your Leo as they are, warts and all, you can't actually be in love with them, you're in love with an image of them.

I see this so much in my private practice and it's the saddest thing about relationships.

The point I am making is, you really don't need your Leo to *care* about your feelings, which they do and will; what you really want is for your Leo to *acknowledge* your feelings, and that can be a little trickier.

My advice would be to make a deal with your Leo that once a month you will actually talk about and agree on things that make you feel better. If you prefer to have time to yourself, and not to be accused of ignoring your Leo, then say so. Leos really don't like being ignored or left out of things, so if you're someone that needs a lot of 'alone' time, *make sure you explain this to your Leo and agree on it.*

I had a female Leo client who was convinced her Aries

boyfriend didn't care about her feelings. She was drinking vast amounts of coffee and suffering from PMT. When I heard the full story, I thought, if I was Mr Aries I'd be scared about her 'feelings' as they were so in-your-face, constant and tiring.

I explained that Mr Aries probably cared deeply for her, but she would have to do some work on not being so dramatic all of the time, and to stay off the coffee for a few weeks and see if that made a difference. It's uncanny how too much coffee sets your emotions into overdrive and certainly doesn't make for a peaceful, contented lifestyle.

Chapter Seven

The Solutions

Now that you know a little more about what type of Leo is in your life, you can work a bit smarter on how to get along with them better.

As the title of this book promises, you're going to learn how to lavish your Leo as lavish is the word that really makes them feel happy. In fact the title of the book was suggested by a young Leo lady called Louise I worked with, so full credit goes to her.

My trusty dictionary defines lavish as: *bestow or spend money, effort, praise etc. abundantly.*

The key word here is 'abundant'. It's no good saying something nice and flattering to your Leo once a year. That certainly isn't abundant! But were you to remind them quite a few times a day how lovely they are, or how much they've helped you do something, or how grateful you are for their input or advice, your Leo will be purring contentedly and all will be well with the world.

One thing you mustn't do is ignore them.

Here are what a few Leos have told me they would do/feel if they were ignored:

I would ignore them back! Unless I wanted to speak to them, then I would approach them.

I would ask that person if something was wrong and let them know how I feel.

I would feel very frustrated and upset, wondering what I had done or said to make them behave that way... even if I knew the reason and thought it were my fault, I would still feel that way. I would feel impatient to find a way to make them get in contact. I would feel disappointed and sad if it were someone I cared about. If it were a stranger I would feel annoyed that they had been rude.

I don't like it, I wish after the event I had gone up and said hi.

Depends who it is – if it is someone I care about it would be upsetting.

I guess it would tick me off first but I would get over it. This happens very seldom to me.

I would think that they didn't have anything to say to me or for me to say to them. I will usually try to make contact to find out what the problem is. I do look a little 'exotic' so understand that not everyone finds my look welcoming.

As you can grasp from the above quotes, it's not something that a) happens often to a Leo or b) makes them feel good.

So if your Leo is upset about something or racing around the house, sighing and wailing and causing a fuss, or acting rather grumpy and out-of-sorts, take their Moon or Ascendant sign into account and tailor your help as below.

Also, remember to use the Bach Flower Essences if things are really bad and it looks as if your Leo is going to go all wobbly.

Aries Asc or Moon

Being soft and gentle is not what is needed here. Lots of physical action, an energetic solution that involves pushing the body to extremes will work best. Tai Chi, Squash, Rugby, anything where they can compete and beat the pants off you. Hopefully you'll survive the onslaught, so be prepared for some fast and lively experiences to help them fight off their feelings.

Taurus Asc or Moon

Slow, steady planning is needed here. To make your Leo/Taurus feel better you will need tasty well-cooked, value-for-money food, some fine wine and lots and lots of time. They will love you forever if you offer a massage or body treatment and will happily enjoy reconnecting with their body.

Gemini Asc or Moon

If your Leo has a Gemini combination, they will feel better if they can talk, talk, talk. It's no good offering advice without allowing them the chance to 'speak their truth'. I've found also that this combo feels better if you take them out for a short journey in the car, and they're likely to tell you far more than if you were face-to-face. You can also suggest a good book to read on whatever subject is causing the drama.

Cancer Asc or Moon

No one with a Cancer dominated chart feels good if they can't touch and embrace and hug when they're feeling out of sorts. There's so much you can do to make them feel better just by giving them a hug. If you or they have some friendly pets, get them involved too. Plus keep a big box of tissues handy as this combo can cry for England and some more; so don't do the stiff-upper-lip thing with them, it won't work. Expect lots of tears and then later laughter when they've cried themselves dry.

Leo Asc or Moon

Now you will need to be the director of the play called 'My Leo'. Get them to act out exactly what's happening, how they felt, what they did or didn't do. Do NOT ignore them; this is the time when they need you the most, so giving them the cold shoulder will push them away. Give them the stage, and you will have to be the adoring audience until they've recovered their sense of self.

Virgo Asc or Moon

A Leo with Virgo bits will worry, then they will worry some more, then they will worry that they're worrying... and the whole thing will go round and round in circles. You will have to be firm and get them to lie down in a darkened room for a while and let them switch off mentally. Yoga, meditation and calm company are what they need. They might demand the doctor, and provided it's necessary, do just that but keep in mind they're capable of exaggeration, so try some calming techniques first.

Libra Asc or Moon

Libra Leos will want everything to be fair and balanced, which you and I know is not realistic. They will fret if there are too many options and too much to think about, so reduce the current problems to 'that which is most important' and concentrate on that first. If you surround them with pastel colours, nice furnishings, delicate and dainty details, they will calm down enough to tell you what's happening. Do not give too many choices, or they'll be off again.

Scorpio Asc or Moon

As this is the most deep and transformational sign combo, light and fluffy solutions won't work. Imagine deep blood red (as a colour, not an image) you will get more of an idea of what will work. They will want to 'do' drastic things, so suggest meaningful remedies like writing and burning a letter to the people/issues concerned or lighting a candle and praying for assistance. Be aware they might take drastic action, so stay out of the firing line if they're really worked-up. This book was written to help the Leo friend, not put them at risk. There is nothing you can say to make things better, so don't bother. Better to be at the end of the phone if they need you and wait until they've completed the suggested tasks.

Sagittarius Asc or Moon

Get out the Bible or relevant book of spiritual authority. Help them choose a passage that relates to what's happening to them at the moment. They want to believe that what they've done or are doing is 'right' so arguing won't work. If you have the money, book a nice foreign trek somewhere exciting; this will keep them busy until they feel better as this combo loves long distant travel.

Capricorn Asc or Moon

You will need the advice of an 'Elder' here, so anyone you know who is older and wiser than your Cap/Leo will be good. Get them to take your Cap/Leo to one side and describe how they got out of the sticky situation your Leo is in. They want someone who is serious and sensible with practical solutions. Visiting an ancient site or old building like a stately home will also help.

Aquarius Asc or Moon

Any ideas you may have that have the words 'new ideas', 'freedom', 'radical change' or just plain 'weird' will appeal. As this is the combo that loves mental freedom So Much, all you have to do is not restrict them, not tie-them-down, not curtail their wonderful ideas in any way. They want to feel part of some altruistic solution, which benefits mankind (and them in the process), so going on a march to 'save the whales' or anything to do with Greenpeace will be good. They want to feel inspired and excited about their nirvana.

Pisces Asc or Moon

As this is the sign combo that communicates with fairies, angels and other beings of light, you will need to take them to an astrologer or psychic, not the bank manager. They will want to burn incense, dream the afternoon away, feel part of the higher dimensions that they love so much. When they're a little more grounded you can talk practical matters, but for starters, go for the mind-body-spirit solution.

Chapter Eight

Lavishing Skills

We're now going to fine-tune all the advice I've given so far. We're also going to learn about the different Leos that you'll come across in everyday life. As this is a practical book, I will be giving practical solutions you can use yourself and I've divided it into the various individuals that we all come across.

Your Leo Child

Generally speaking, Leos *love* to be children. They enjoy the whole childhood thing. Being excited about Christmas, being in the spotlight at family functions, loving animals and music and dance. They can be very creative and there are a vast number of artists, musicians, dancers, singers and performers who are Leos.

You cannot give a Leo child too much attention. They will lap it up. What sign you are will determine if you find parenting your Leo child easy or challenging.

Air or Fire signs generally find it easier. Water and Earth sign parents might find that they don't quite understand all the drama all the time, unless, of course, they've got Leo Ascendants or Moons themselves. This makes the job a lot easier.

As Leo is a fixed sign, and one that doesn't like too much change, your Leo child will feel happier if you don't move house too much, or make them change schools (unless they ask).

Nadine is the Pisces Mum and witch that we met earlier. Here she tells us about parenting her Leo daughter:

Leos make lovely, bouncy, sunny children. They are loving and very tactile – always up for a hug or painting toenails! They have a huge capacity for seeing the positive, pointing out the obvious and counting their blessings.

An unhappy Leo can be a confused little character, they really cannot see what has gone wrong to oust them from their happy place. Nurture, cuddles and some suggestions of what to do next can really help, but they need to work it out for themselves... all the advice in the world won't make their next steps obvious!

Overall though having a little Leo in your world is a blessing, their sunny smiles can really make your day!

Willow is a Gemini author who lives and works in Surrey, UK:

I'm quite sure that my Leo daughter was talking to me in the womb and she hasn't stopped since! (She wanted plenty of room for herself and didn't like me eating big meals.)

She was obviously a social child right from the start. I handed her over to all hospital visitors and she was perfectly happy communicating with them. When newborn, I'd sit with her on my lap while the sun shone through the window and she'd spread out totally relaxed, pouting her lips in bliss! She has craved the sun ever since and now lives in southern Spain.

She has always drawn people in who would do anything for her and she doesn't need to prove herself. I'd pick her up from nursery and watch the teacher buttoning up her coat, even though she could do it herself. It was the attention she liked!

At seven she came home from school unhappy because friends were calling her a show-off. I asked her if she was showing off and she said, 'Yes!'

So I said, 'Well, you can either stop showing off or you can carry on and accept the name calling.'

She thought about it and decided she'd rather carry on showing off!

As a mum of a Leo child I am blessed to have received as much love back as I have given to her. And who couldn't love her? She is fun-loving, generous and kind and her many friends are loyal in return.

Bernadette is an Aquarius mother and creative writer who has a Leo son called Luke. Here she talks about what he was like when he was little:

He liked to wear odd combinations of clothes and especially hats, sometimes two at once. He also liked taking his clothes off and for most of his early childhood he didn't wear much at all. He wasn't brilliant at talking as his speech was garbled but he liked to communicate and he liked stories.

He had favourite stories he wanted read again and again. He was fascinated with steam trains and when we lived in Devon we sometimes went up and down all day on the local steam train. He had a terrible temper and would scream and throw himself on the floor if he didn't want to do something.

He had an amazing imagination and he played for hours in the garden talking to himself and his invisible friends. He had three invisible friends, Bic, Diggory and Cuckoo and he had long and lasting conversations with them. He made up very complex games and also made things out of boxes and sticky tape, such as houses and cars.

Until he was about four he didn't really have any particular friends. Although he liked playing with other kids he didn't remember who they were or even knew their names, which I thought was odd. He certainly wanted other children to join in 'his game'.

When we moved to the South West I think he missed having loads of outdoor space as he was always happiest outdoors. He didn't really like the local school and didn't fit in with the kids there so we sent him to the Waldorf school and he absolutely flourished. Everybody loved him. Everybody loves Luke!!!!

He is open and friendly and upbeat and positive and says what he feels and is encouraging to people who are less confident than him. At the Waldorf school he met his best friend Thor, and they have been friends ever since. With his younger brothers he has always been the 'Big Brother' and he got them to do tasks for him, such as tidying up his room. He was in charge of the games and he often played one brother off against the other. He has a sentimental streak and had a teddy until he was nearly a teenager.

Luke did well at the Waldorf School as they had plenty of acting and art, which he is good at both. He also went to the TV drama school for a while and got a few bit parts in various TV productions. At one point I thought he was going to be an actor but he decided against this as he thought the other actors were too self-involved. Ever since he started school he has had an active and huge social circle and he still has simply heaps of friends.

I suppose that being a mother to Luke was like being in the audience and clapping every time he did something. He wanted lots of praise and applause and he thrived on it. He didn't like rules or being tidy or thinking about things in advance or being told what to do and if we had arguments it was usually around these issues.

In these very full accounts of mothering a Leo child, Bernadette gives us quite a good idea of the themes involved. When he didn't want to do something, he'd scream and throw himself on the floor. It's pointless making any fixed sign 'do' something they don't want to do. The only way around it is to make the unwanted thing appealing in some way. You also have to be pretty firm when tantrums do occur. Telling them to stop only makes them worse. Ignoring them, the tantrums that is, not the child, takes the energy out of them.

The Bach Flower remedies work really well, so does Emotional Freedom Technique (EFT) – things you can do at home – or taking your child to a Homeopath, Acupuncturist, Osteopath or other Alternative therapist.

Notice, also, how when he liked to do something, he did it over and over. Fixed signs like the familiarity of things they enjoy. It gives them pleasure, so why not? The mutable signs of Gemini, Virgo, Sagittarius and Pisces would go bonkers if you did the same thing all the time, and the cardinal signs would wonder why you weren't going on to another level or progressing with a game or sport.

A fixed sign is happy being at whatever level they are in a game or sport; that brings them joy and they will be very reticent to alter that nice feeling. Unless, of course, they were in a competitive environment; then they would try very hard to 'reach for gold'.

I liked how Bernadette told us how Luke made his younger brothers tidy up for him. How Leo! To be waited on hand and foot! Luckily Luke's brothers are both Water signs. I don't think he'd have had such luck if they'd been Air or Fire signs; he would have had an argument or fight on his hands!

I also liked how Willow's daughter was asked to make a choice between being called names and stopping showing off, and she chose to show-off and ignore the name calling. Wise parenting skills involved there from an Air sign.

Your Leo Boss

Having a Leo boss isn't always a smooth ride. It does, as always, depend on what sign and element you are, and also how you feel about having a boss.

If your skills and experience are similar, or the same as your Leo boss, the match will not be made in heaven, because they won't be able to advise or guide you, as you know as much as they do already. So having a partnership (if you're self-employed) with a Leo is not a good idea, as the concept of sharing or doing things in a shared way won't always cross your Leo's mind.

If you work for a large organisation, and your Leo boss has worked his way up to his/her position, there is more chance for your work relationship to be better.

Your Leo boss will see you as the beginner, as the newbie and they'll take you under their wing and guide you on your path. They will expect and enjoy lots of thanks and praise for their magnanimity and all will be well... until you ask for a promotion. Then I'm afraid the only tactic that works would be flattery.

If you want promotion, you're better off appealing to the cardinal signs in your place of work (Aries, Cancer, Libra & Capricorn) as they're looking into the future far more than the fixed signs... who as I've mentioned more than once, don't like change. And for you to ask for promotion involves change.

Two examples of a (male) Leo boss that have made the news come to mind.

And both of them have interesting Astrological associations.

Bill Clinton, the 42nd president of the USA, is a Leo with Libra Ascendant and Moon in Taurus. Both his Sun and Moon are in fixed signs. In 1995 Monica Lewinsky was hired as an intern at the White House while Bill was president. I won't go into the full story, as there is something far more interesting about the incident.

Monica is *also* a Leo, *also* with Libra Ascendant and *also* with Moon in Taurus.

Hugo Chávez became president of the country Venezuela that lies on the north coast of South America in 1999. He is heavily influenced by someone called Simon Bolivar who died 124 years before he was born, even going as far as to have his remains exhumed and commissioning a 3-D lifelike statue of the man.[12]

This doesn't really make any sense, until you check their birth charts, and Hugo and Simon share the same Sun sign of Leo, the same Mercury sign of Cancer, the same Venus sign of Virgo and their two outer planets of Uranus (which takes 80+ years to go through the Zodiac) and even more spookily the same Neptune sign of Libra (which takes over 100 years to orbit the Earth).

Here we have a typical Leo boss, wanting recognition and praise and even going as far as bringing on board someone who clearly can't physically influence the proceedings but that feeling of empathy comes from somewhere. From their astrological horoscope similarities.

On a good day your Leo boss will encourage you, praise you, do all of the things he/she would like him/herself. On a bad day they might fly into a rage, shout, get all worked-up when he/she feels you don't support, love or respect him/her.

Your Leo Friend

Your Leo friend will be loyal, supportive, loving and warm, provided you are equally loyal, supportive, loving and warm. We all like to give what we receive and Leo is no different.

Veronique is a Gemini who lives in Somerset. She's semi-retired and works with clients using flower essences and counselling.

She has two Leo friends:

Both my Leo friends are wonderful people, with strong but different spiritual beliefs, and among my very dearest friends. I realised recently that they both are capable of bringing sunshine into others' lives and inspiring, empowering or enabling others by their very special glow. They both give the most excellent attention when someone is talking to them, so conversation is very much a 50:50 thing (this may not be all that typical of your average Leo!). But then, they are both counsellors and healers. Creative themselves, they can also inspire others, one in terms of creativity, and one to act lovingly towards others in every situation. Both are loved – adored even – by their friends, who value them very highly.

Kristina is also a Gemini and is a student of creative writing and lives in Eastern Europe. She has Leo friends:

A Leo friend is loyal. NOT reliable, Aries is reliable. Leo is loyal. He will not always rush to help right away when you need it (Aries will), but he will always defend you in any way possible and stand by you through anything. And they demand the same loyalty from others, a Leo will not tolerate a betrayal, you will then have an enemy for life.

I have had a number of Leo friends over the years, sadly two of them died recently; but they were always fun to be with, had a sparkling sense of humour, were concerned always with the underdog (both of them were musicians/singer-songwriters) and would write songs about funny happenings or to help others like worthy causes.

To keep on the best side of your Leo friend, make sure you acknowledge the things that are helpful to/for you, and ignore any dramatic displays of emotion. They will love surprise birthday parties and anything that has a certain amount of drama in it. If you're a Water or Earth sign, don't spend too much time together, otherwise the relationship will grate and you'll end up falling-out. If you have any planets in Leo or a Leo Ascendant, things will progress much more smoothly.

Your Leo (female) Lover

To successfully date a Leo lady, you will need to know a few things that they enjoy, and do those things for, or with, your Leo. Keeping in mind what sign and element you are will also assist your dating success.

To make things easier for you, I've included here a few ideas of what makes a Leo female tick, and also how they would like to be lavished. As this is, after all, their siren cry.

Here we have Hattie; How would you like to be lavished?

Wow! What a question!

Even asking the question has made her feel good!...

Whisked away in a private jet with my 'perfect' man to a tropical island, where we are waited on hand and foot with amazing food and drinks, and massaged and pampered to our hearts' content.

60

I think this succinctly sums up a typical Leo female lavishing tactic, but let's explore a few other ladies' suggestions. Each of them was asked the question: 'How would you like to be lavished?' Don't forget, the word in the title of this book was suggested by a Leo, so the word itself is indicative of Leo attributes.

Here is Clarissa:

A country retreat with my 3 daughters where we can have spa time, good food and quality time away from ALL electronics.

Laura the graphic designer from New Zealand also has a good idea of what sort of lavishing she'd like:

With nice, good quality, perhaps even expensive clothes, taken out for an amazing meal with special attention to dessert, perhaps some sparkly champagne or cocktails to go with it... followed by an entertaining evening with music and fun. At the moment I am very excited to see Cirque du Soleil. My 30th birthday is approaching and I have been very concerned to find something lavish and amazing and memorable to celebrate it! This is what I chose!

Notice how she wants to celebrate her birthday. Leo must be the only sign that truly enjoys birthdays. It doesn't matter how old they get, they still enjoy their special day, being pampered, being special, having everyone wish them good cheer. Unlike a Gemini, who hates birthdays and generally changes their date of birth the older they get so no one actually knows how old they are, or Capricorn that views each birthday as one more piece of evidence that life is finite, or Pisces that tends to forget they've got a birthday coming up until it's too late to invite people to celebrate...

One Leo lady housewife called Julie, who is in her 70s, when asked just gave one short answer, but look at how exotic that answer was:

Taken on safari.

Not like a Sagittarius who would say 'go on safari', this was 'taken' as in being accompanied and treated to the safari!

Then there was Diane who simply wanted:

To be driven to a nice meal out and a trip to the theatre.

Notice how she says 'nice' meal, implying that eating in a burger bar wouldn't quite live up to expectation. And a trip to the theatre is a good Leo treat as the theatre is all about entertainment and being amused. Also, 'driven', because ladies do not drive *themselves* on a date!

Leos want something where they don't have to 'do' anything other than lap up the joy. More suggestions here:

Getting pampered with massages and bodywork. Taking a nice long vacation. Just being able to rest and taking care of myself is lavishing to me.

I would like to be surprised by a trip to somewhere in the country or by the sea to have a lovely day out with great food and not have to worry about money.

Being pampered, surprised, treated, made to feel special are all top of the list for Leo ladies.

Another way, other than asking directly, to find out what a Leo woman wants is to read the dating websites and pay close attention to the requests. When people are looking for a partner, they tend to write mostly about themselves, not what they're actually looking for, so it gives more of an insight into the sign itself.

Here is a young lady on a UK dating website:

I don't have a preference of what job you do (as long as you have one), I'm not hugely bothered what your hobbies are (as long as you have some) and I don't really mind where you're from (although I do go a bit gooey-eyed for a Northern boy).

I suppose what I'm looking for is someone who's worked out who they are, who's confident and a maybe a little self-assured... Who's man enough to know what he wants (preferably me) and not scared to go out and get it.

So, to date a Leo lady successfully you will need to be earning money (so you can spend it on her), have a hobby (so you can show her off to your friends), be confident and self-assured. Aren't these qualities we've already discovered that a Leo will have in abundance anyway?

What you will also have to have is: lots of patience, so you can deal with the dramas when they happen; a listening ear, so you can hear all the wonderful things they've been doing and are planning; and an ability to be firm but remaining respectful if they get too bossy or self-centred.

This young lady describes some typical Leo likes and interests:

I am a make-up artist; I work in fashion, advertising and music. I love to cook and to eat good food particularly sushi!! I enjoy travelling, friends, film, bikram yoga, cycling, running and healthy living with a couple of unhealthy days a week thrown in!

I love art, fashion, interiors, kids, small furry creatures and some big ones, although that doesn't include men with an abundance of body hair. I am looking for somebody who is confident, open-minded, young at heart, creative, who enjoys music, film, festivals and food, food, food... someone interested in cooking, eating and travel!

A sense of adventure and a bit of spontaneity is pretty important too along with a decent sense of humour.

Your Leo (male) Lover

Dating and finding love with a Leo man is slightly different from the female perspective. I think it's because, as Leo is represented by the male lion, as opposed to the lioness, there's an expectation that the Leo gentleman will want to be more aggressive emotionally, more demonstrative... when in real life there is no difference.

Both sexes want permanent and lasting love.

Pisces Nadine gives us her thoughts:

In a perfect world a Leo would be seated on a pedestal and fed grapes! In my experience Leo partners love to be the instigators, the problem solvers and the knights in shining armour. This can obviously be a problem if you yourself are a freethinking individual who loves to be spontaneous!

Not all Leo men are swashbuckling 'he' men. Sometimes there's a more subtle side to them.

Grant is a Leo man who lives and works in London as a network systems analyst. He tells me his feelings about being lavished, and he's realised it's not about 'things' but about true feelings:

These days there's only one thing I really need – acknowledgement. If I tell someone something, or if I send them a card or e-mail, or if I make the effort to spend some time with them – I don't want to be ignored. I find it very disconcerting to say something to my colleagues at work and be met by a blank look, or just to move the conversation on. Likely I am too deep (or dry) for them but I would much prefer someone just looked me in the eye and said 'Don't understand' or even just nodded / smiled in my direction. If you ever want to really get rid of a Leo just don't give them any reaction. If we do cross each other's paths and we do interact – just don't ignore or blank me. My regal Sun and Moon in Leo feels incredibly bothered by that.

This is the crux of the Leo psyche's deepest need: To be acknowl-edged. So keep that in mind if you're dating a Leo man.

Here is Kristina again:

You CAN NOT outshine a Leo lover. NEVER. Let him be the star, the most important, at the center of attention, be the protector and in a certain way even the 'owner', let everyone know and see that you are with him, that you are HIS lady. And in return you will get the most gentle and the most caring man there can possibly be. While you let him shine in public, you will be the star when alone with him. One thing they really know how to do is make a woman feel like she is the only one in the whole world, the most beautiful and desired one.

Karen is a Virgo herbalist and lives in Georgia, USA. She is married to Steve who runs a car dealership.

Our story is one that has a lot of people 'aww-ing'. Long-story-short: We met on a bus at the 1996 Paralympic Games in Atlanta – he lived a 7-hour drive away. Although I was making eyes at his friend, the friend ensured we sat together at dinner and then drinks after dinner. Tom (the friend) was right – for once. It was more-or-less 'love at first sight' but it took him 2 weeks to figure it out – after talking with both his mother and closest friend.

The proposal? We were on one of our 3-hour-every-night calls, discussing his moving in with me and the wedding. I told him he'd never asked the question. What followed was 'wanna?'

I said 'of course' and we got back to the conversation.

Our wedding was a year and a few days after we met. Although my mother figured at our ages we'd just live together, we both wanted to make it legal. The only reason we didn't just go to a judge as soon as he relocated was because I wanted the wedding I didn't get the first time. We were married in a civil ceremony on the banks of the Chattahoochee River at a restaurant/bar that had been my 'hang out' for many years. A few close friends joined us there & in the restaurant afterward for dinner. After that, we partied in the bar – and we were the last to leave.

There's no doubt that a Leo man can be romantic and loving. You don't have to 'be' anything special to make him interested in you; just be interested in him and you'll be fine.

Back at the dating sites two gentlemen were looking for love. This gentleman reduced it down to three words:

Not too serious maybe, sees life as opportunity and fun – and the 3 f's – funny, fit and fabulous.

This gentleman gave a detailed description about himself. How he races BMX for a UK factory team, loves extreme sports, is Italian 'through and through', is also a personal chef and 'absolutely loves music' and the books he is reading at the moment:

What or Who am I looking for? I don't know really, that's why I am here but, I guess, someone kind, independent, loyal, into sports, a passion for travel…

The list could go on but I hate lists, if it would only take a 'shopping' list to find a girlfriend I would probably go to M&S or John Lewis ;-)

Who knows where this will take me or who will I meet along the way? Keeping a positive outlook is, well, essential :-)

Well, apart from what I wrote above, it's all down to that elusive click. The chemistry so to speak.

Lists are no good when looking for a soul mate!

So, if you like the sound and the look of my profile, get in touch.

As you will note, he's more interested in you liking him, than him liking you (!!) as his description of himself was very lengthy. It was interesting how he didn't specify what he'd be able to *offer* any potential partner; neither did any of the other Leo profiles that I read.

Best thing to keep in mind is, if you find a Leo attractive or appealing, just that in itself will be enough to provoke some rapport.

What to do if your Leo relationship ends

If your relationship with your Leo ends, you must keep in mind your own Element to deal with the pain.

Generally Leos don't like it when relationships finish. They're quite set in their ways and will hang on in there, even though they might not be happy. It's more likely that you will end the relationship than them.

Fire Sign

If you are a Fire sign: Aries, Leo or Sagittarius, you will need something active and dynamic to help you get over your relationship ending. You will need the element of fire in your healing process. Get a nice nightlight candle and light it and recite:

I... (your name) do let you... (Leo's name) go, in freedom and with love so that I am free to attract my true soul-love.

Leave the nightlight in a safe place to completely burn away. Allow at least an hour. In the meantime gather up any belongings or possessions that are your (now) ex-lover's and deliver them back to your Leo. It's polite to telephone first and notify your ex when you will be arriving.

If you have any photos of you together or other mementos or even gifts, don't be in a big rush to destroy them, as some Fire signs are prone to do. Better to put them away in a box in the attic or garage until you feel a little less upset.

In a few months' time go through the box and keep the things you like and give away the things you don't.

Earth Sign

If you are an Earth sign: Taurus or Virgo or Capricorn, you will feel less inclined to do something dramatic or outrageous. It might also take you slightly longer to recover your equilibrium, so allow yourself a few weeks and a maximum of three months to grieve. You will be using the earth element to help your healing and some crystals. The best crystals to use are the ones associated with your Sun sign and also with protection.

Taurus = Emerald

Virgo = Agate

Capricorn = Onyx

Cleanse your crystal in fresh running water. Wrap it in some pretty silk fabric, and then go on a walk into the countryside. When you find a suitable spot, that is quiet and where you won't be disturbed, dig a small hole and place your crystal in the ground.

Spend a few minutes thinking about your relationship, the good times and the bad. Forgive yourself for any mistakes you may have made. Imagine a beautiful plant emerging from the ground where you have buried your crystal, and the plant blossoming and growing strong.

This will represent your new love that will be with you when the time is right.

Air Sign

If you're an Air sign: Gemini, Libra or Aquarius, you might want to talk about what happened first before you finish the relationship. Air signs need reasons and answers, and can waste precious life-energy looking for 'the reason why'. You might need to meet with your Leo to tell him/her exactly what you think/thought about his/her opinions, ideas and thoughts. You might also be tempted to tell him/her what you think about them now, which I do not recommend.

Far better to put those thoughts into a tangible form by writing your ex-Leo a letter. It is not a letter that you are actually going to post, but you are going to put as much energy into writing it *as if* you were going to send it.

Write to them thus:

Dear Leo,
I expect you will be happy now in your new life, but there are a few things I would like you to know and understand before I say goodbye.

Then list all the annoying, aggravating, upsetting ideas that your (now) ex-Leo indulged in. Make a list as long as you like. Put in as much detail as you feel comfortable with, including things like how many times they upstaged you, or showed off in front of your family, or went overboard with the drama. Keep writing till you can write no more, then end your letter with something such as:

Even though we were not suited, and I suffered because of this, I wish you well on your path.

Or some other positive comment.

Then tear your letter into teeny little pieces and put them into a small container. We are now going to use the element of air to rectify the situation. Take a trip to somewhere windy and high, like the top of the hill, and when you're ready open your container and sprinkle a *few* random pieces of your letter into the wind. Don't use the entire letter or you run the risk of littering; just enough pieces to be significant.

Watch those little pieces of paper fly into the distance and imagine them connecting with the nature spirits.

Your relationship has now ended.

Water Sign

If you are a Water sign: Cancer, Scorpio or Pisces, you might find it more difficult to recover quickly from your relationship. You might find yourself weeping at inopportune moments, or when you hear 'your' song on the radio, or when you see other couples happily being in each other's company. You might lie awake at night worrying that you have ruined your life and your ex-Leo is having all the fun. As you might have gathered by now, this is unlikely. Your ex might be as upset as you.

Your emotional healing therefore needs to incorporate the water element.

As you are capable of weeping for the World, the next time you are in floods of tears capture one small teardrop and place it into a small glass. Have one handy just for this purpose. Decorate it if you feel like it with small flowers, stars, or twinkly things.

Now fill your glass to the top with tap water and place it on a table.

Then recite the following:

This loving relationship with you... (Leo's name) *has ended.*
I reach out across time and space to you.
My tears will wash away the hurt I feel.
I release you from my heart, mind and soul.
We part in peace.

And then slowly drink the water. Imagine your hurt dissolving away, freeing you from all the anxieties you feel and releasing you from the deep sadness. Then spend the next few weeks being nice to yourself. If you need to talk, find someone you trust and confide in them. Keep tissues handy.

Your Leo Mum/Mom

I know quite a few Leo Mums. They're very devoted and protective of their children and since Leo is the sign of childhood and creation, they enjoy their children especially when they're young, as there's more fun to be had.

When I was very young I knew a lovely Leo Mum. She was a wonderful cook, a super friendly person and couldn't, like lots of Leos, say 'No'.

She had four children of her own, but she very kindly took me in to live with her when I wanted to come back to the UK while my parents were abroad. She put me up for more than a year and never once lost her temper with me, even though, looking back, I must have been the teen-lodger-from-hell.

I smoked, I stayed out late, I was always on the phone (this was years before mobile phones), I put clothes into wash even though I'd only worn them once and the only time she 'had a word with me' was when I'd put *all* my clothes into wash and she couldn't find anything dirty about them... (I was too lazy to put them away).

She'd had a troubled childhood and made her home into a sort of mini crisis centre, homing stray dogs and cats that turned up and caring for her husband's relatives when they visited from abroad. One in-law relative was studying for a degree and went through an awful psychotic episode but she cared for him, talking late into the night and making him feel valued and loved.

We used to spend late nights together, when she would tell me all about her troubled childhood and in a way I'm glad I listened (I was very happy to), if only to pay her back for all her kindness.

If any of her children were in trouble, she wouldn't think twice to rush to them and try and help.

She was a wonderful woman and sadly died early of cancer. Maybe she was too caring...

Not everyone likes that level of attention, and if you're a more

independent sign, you might find having a Leo Mum can be a bit
tiresome:

*I'm Aquarius, (Aries Moon and Ascendant) and ever since I was a
kid I liked being independent and doing my own thing.*

*Recently my mom and I had an argument and I told her 'just let
me live my own **** life!' and she got really upset by that and said
that we couldn't live as a family when everyone is insisting that they
should live their own lives (me and my father).*

*I feel as though she's clinging onto me. She always compares me
to my father (a Sagittarius) and blames us for wanting to do things
our own way. I mean, I don't know any other way to live. This is
how I am. Am I wrong for insisting that she should just let me be?*

*I think she expects people to depend on each other so much. I'm
so confused. I mean her imperfections aside I still I love my mom,
but I also like being free.*

Goodness me! What a terrible dilemma for an Aquarius. I had it
the other way round. My mother is an Aquarius and gave us pots
of freedom when we were young, and couldn't *wait* for us to leave
home. And here we have the astrological dilemma of opposite
signs.

Aquarius is all about freedom, so is Sagittarius (see my books
How to Bond with an Aquarius and *How to Believe in a Sagittarius*)
and Leo is all about being needed. The freedom Aquarius is
looking for though is mental freedom. Sagittarius is looking for
physical freedom. This household would certainly operate better
if this Leo Mom allowed her daughter to just 'be', without prying
into her thought processes and 'whys'. In a situation like this, it
certainly helps if Leo Mom has interests other than her family.
Maybe join a dance or drama class, or do volunteer work, because
eventually the child/ren will leave home and she'll be out of a job.

As a general rule, Leo Mums love their children. They are now
part of their pack, their tribe, their pride. And pride is what they

want to feel. They want to feel proud that their child has done well *because* of their mothering.

Your Leo Dad

A Leo father can be all of the qualities we've talked about already – or not. If you're lucky he will be optimistic, magnanimous, caring and full of fun.

If you're a Fire sign and provided there is nothing negative going on with your Moons – you should get on well.

I know a number of Leo Dads and also people with Leo fathers and most of them don't complain too much about their parent.

Here is Janice, who is a Virgo, describing the good relationship she had with both her Leo parents:

My 7th House is Leo, and both my parents were Leos. I took care of my parents at the end of their lives, and they were my best friends. My Leo father died in his and my home, my mother died in a home that belonged to her and I. I had the option of putting them, as many do, in a residential retirement home, but I couldn't do it.

Sometimes people remember their parents fondly and get on with them really well. Here is Heather, a Gemini financial manager in the city of London.

I loved my Leo father to bits. He was kind, caring and protective. He was sociable, funny and a bit bombastic. He was loyal, brave and also very sensitive. He was always there for me and my sister. We stayed in a hotel on the Isle of Wight on my last family holiday. My sister and I were in a room together and my parents were in a room along the hall. I was 15 and my sister was 12, so when a team of drunken rugby players came along the hall looking for our room, I was a bit scared. My father came out of his room, all 5'6" of him (and dressed in his underwear) and told several tall young men to 'go away', which of course they did.

I was so proud of him that night.

My father was the person who saw how directionless I was at 16, took me to the City of London to get a job and set me on the path of a lifelong career. He helped me decorate and furnish numerous homes, even though he was rubbish at DIY and he took me in when my first marriage ended. He was there to listen, advise and occasionally criticise, but he always had my best interests at heart. He was my best friend and there is never a day goes by when I don't miss him.

However, if you're an Earth or Water sign, things might be a bit more tricky.

Clarissa is an author and very concerned about the welfare of the planet and its resources. She is a Taurus. Here she is talking about her Leo Dad:

My relationship with my Leo father was not an easy or straight-forward one. Nor, from the little I know about astrology, does it seem to me that he was a typical Leo.

Accountant to a large estate all his life, a dedicated gardener and keen golfer, my Dad was conservative, quiet and thoughtful, and essentially a solitary soul. Nor was he emotionally open, which was probably exacerbated by the early loss of his firstborn son. From what I can remember of him as a child – many memories were blocked by the death of my older brother – my father seemed very stern with high expectations. I was always a little afraid of him and never really felt we could relate on any level, which went on until he died. I did, however, love the way he walked – very gracefully, like a dancer. Not a handyman in any respect, he nevertheless inspired me with his ergonomic organisational abilities and his meticulousness, and his dedication to 'doing the best you can, simply because you are doing it'. He died when I was thirty, and there has always remained in me a regret that we never really connected. Yet I still feel a deep and abiding love for him.

While he resignedly accepted them, he never tried to understand my choices in life. Today, my mother says he was afraid of me! I do remember trying to talk with him in my late teens/early twenties, when I tried to understand socialism and communism (!) but how can you debate with someone for whom you have an innate respect and who simply dismisses your ideas as lack of experience?

Clarissa's father definitely was a Leo, but he had Moon in Virgo and a very clustered chart. He also had Saturn (the planet of responsibility) right next to his Sun sign, so it sounds as if he was weighed down with responsibility and the death of his only son and that took away some of his spark. He also wouldn't have wanted to hear about political issues, when she's already said he was a dedicated gardener and golfer. I expect he would have felt better talking about his gardening and the things that interested him, than things he would never experience like 'socialism'.

Your Leo father will want to give you advice, expect you to follow it, be concerned for your welfare and will especially want to feel proud of something you've achieved.

Your Leo Sibling

I don't have a Leo sibling, so what I'm going to tell you is not from my own personal experience. I do, however, know a number of people who have a Leo sibling, and like with Leo Dad and Mum it all depends on what sign and Element you are.

If you are both Leos, there will have to be an agreement about who is 'leader of the pack', as one of you will have to be the 'boss' and the other the 'employee' or follower. It's difficult for any relationship to work if both of you are in the driving seat. Someone has to be the passenger.

Here is Clarissa again. She also has a Leo sister:

A happy and sunny child, she was the apple of our grandmother's and father's eye. Her relationship with our Leo father was quite different to mine. Maybe he had mellowed by then, or maybe it was because they were both Leo, but she wasn't afraid to stand up to him and even jokily put him down – 'what do you know, you've lived in the same place all your life!' – which made him laugh. I actually used to be amazed at what I saw as her lack of respect, saying things I would never have got away with, but he seemed to like it from her. I loved my little sister and she was very close to me, but then when she was nine I went off to college and then left the country and saw her only two or three times in the next twenty years. As she was definitely not a letter-writer, we really had almost no contact. Yet whenever we did get together – then as well as now – we get on very, very well and have a great laugh and deep sharing, and she has a fair degree of self-awareness. Like our father, she chose one career and stuck to it, and bought a house as soon as she could because – as she put it – she 'couldn't stand the idea of lack of security'. To this day, she hates having to move.

I've made both their charts and Clarissa has Gemini Ascendant, Sun Taurus, Moon Taurus and her sister has Virgo Ascendant, Sun Leo, Moon Virgo, so there is enough shared Earth between their charts to prevent any major fallings-out.

If you're having a hard time with your Leo sibling, check out yours and their charts and look for the connections and focus on them.

If you're Water signs, you might find that your Leo sibling does boss you about. Remember Bernadette and Luke in 'Leo Child', his siblings are Pisces and Cancer and he certainly was the boss. Funnily enough, they never seemed to mind doing things for him, maybe because he was the older brother.

I hope you have enjoyed learning a little astrology and a little about the Sun sign Leo. I am writing this in my home-office in Bath, UK and I have a lit candle next to me and I am sending you light and love and peace for your world.

References

1. *The Astrologers and Their Creed*, Christopher McIntosh, 1971, Arrow Books Ltd, London W1
   The Life and Work of Alan Leo, Bessie Leo, (the Library of the University of California, LA) 1919, LN Fowler & Co, London http://openlibrary.org/

2. *Astronomy*, Paul Sutherland, 2007, Igloo Books Ltd, Sywell, NN6 0BJ

3. *The New Waite's Compendium of Natal Astrology, with Ephemeris for 1880–1980 and Universal Table of Houses*, Colin Evans, revised Brian Gardener, 1967, Routledge & Kegan Paul Ltd, Carter Lane, London

4. *Linda Goodman's Sun Signs*, Linda Goodman, 1976, Pan Books Ltd, London SW10

5. *The Round Art: The Astrology of Time and Space*, AT Mann, 1991, Dragon's World Ltd, Surrey, Great Britain

6. *Astrology, the Stars and Human Life: A Modern Guide*, Christopher McIntosh, 1970, Man, Myth & Magic Original, Macdonald Publishing, Unit 75

7. *Astrology for Dummies*, Rae Orion, 1999, IDG Books Worldwide, Inc., Foster City, CA 94404

8. *The Only Way to Learn Astrology, Volume 1, Basic Principles*, Marion D. March and Joan McEvers, 1995, ACS Publications, San Diego, CA 92123

9. *The Instant Astrologer*, Felix Lyle and Bryan Aspland, 1998, Judy Piatkus Publishers Ltd, London W1

10. "The Decay of Vanity", Ted Hughes, *The Hawk in the Rain*, 1957

11. *How to Read Your Astrological Chart: Aspects of the Cosmic Puzzle*, Donna Cunningham, 1999, Samuel Weiser Inc., York Beach, ME, USA

12. Bolivar reference http://www.bbc.co.uk/news/world-latin-america-18977143

Further Information

The Astrological Association www.astrologicalassociation.com

The Bach Centre, The Dr Edward Bach Centre, Mount Vernon, Bakers Lane, Brightwell-cum-Sotwell, Oxon, OX10 0PZ, UK www.bachcentre.com

Ethical Dating Site www.natural-friends.com

Astrological Chart Information

Chart information and birth data from astro-databank at www.astro.com and www.astrotheme.com

Disputed or unknown time of birth

Enid Blyton, 11th August 1897, London

Elizabeth Queen Mother (UK), 4th August 1900, Moon Scorpio

Madonna, 16th August, 1958

Carl Gustav Jung, 26th July 1875, 7.29pm, Kesswil, Switzerland, Moon Taurus

Stanley Kubrick, 26th July 1928, New York, NY, USA

Kate Bush, 30th July 1958, London, England, Moon Aquarius

Aldous Huxley, 26th July 1894, Godalming, England, Moon Taurus

Emily Brontë, 30th July 1818, Thornton, England, Moon Cancer

JK Rowling, 31st July 1965, Bristol, England, Moon Virgo

Alfred Lord Tennyson, 6th August 1809, Somersby, Lincolnshire, UK, Moon Gemini

Kevin Spacey, 26th July 1959, South Orange, New Jersey, USA, Moon Aries

Marie de Hennezel, 5th August 1946, Lyon, France, Moon Scorpio

The Ascendant

Louis Armstrong, 4th August 1901, New Orleans, LA, USA, 10pm, Aries Ascendant, Sun in 4th, Moon Aries

Mae West, 17th August 1892, 10.30pm, Brooklyn, NY, USA, Taurus Ascendant, Sun in 4th, Moon Cancer

Mick Jagger, 26th July 1943, Dartford, England, 2.30am, Gemini Ascendant, Sun in 2nd, Moon Taurus

Robert De Niro, 17th August 1943, Brooklyn (Kings County), NY, USA, 3am, Cancer Ascendant, Sun in 2nd, Pisces Moon

Andy Warhol, 6th August 1928, 6.30am, Pittsburgh, PA, USA, Leo Ascendant, Sun in 12th, Moon Aries

Roger Federer, 8th August 1981, 8.40am, Basel, Switzerland, Virgo Ascendant, Sun in 12th, Moon Scorpio

Sydney Omarr, 5th August 1926, 11.27am, Philadelphia, PA, USA, Libra Ascendant, Sun in 10th, Moon Cancer

Geri Halliwell, 6th August 1972, 2.30pm, Watford, England, Scorpio Ascendant, Sun in 9th, Moon Cancer

Percy Bysshe Shelley, 4th August, 1792, Horsham, England, 10pm, Taurus Ascendant, Sun in 4th, Moon Pisces

Ted Hughes, 17th August 1930, Mytholmroyd, England, 1.12am, Cancer Ascendant, Sun in 2nd, Moon Taurus

George Bernard Shaw, 26th July 1856, 0.55am, Dublin, Ireland, Gemini Ascendant, Sun in 2nd, Moon Taurus

Alan Leo (born William Frederick Allen), 7th August 1860, London, England, 5.49am, Ascendant Leo, Sun in 12th, Moon Aries

Whitney Houston, 9th August 1963, 8.55pm, Newark, New Jersey, USA, Pisces Ascendant, Sun in 6th, Moon Aries

Barak Obama, 4th August 1961, 7.24pm, Honolulu, HI, USA, Aquarius Ascendant, Sun in 6th, Moon Gemini

Roman Polanski, 18th August 1933, 10.30am, Paris, France, Libra Ascendant, Sun in 11th, Moon Cancer

AT Mann, 18th August 1943, 3.05pm, Auburn, NY, USA, Sagittarius Ascendant, Sun in 9th, Moon Aries

Lucille Ball, 6th August 1911, 5pm, Jamestown, NY, USA, Capricorn Ascendant, Sun in 8th, Moon Capricorn

Martin Sheen, 3rd August 1936, 8.02pm, Dayton, OH, USA, Aquarius Ascendant, Sun in 6th, Moon Leo

Robert Redford, 18th August 1936, 8.02pm, Santa Monica, LA, USA, Pisces Ascendant, Sun in 5th, Moon Virgo

HP Lovecraft, 20th August 1890, 9am, Providence, RI, USA, Libra Ascendant, Sun in 11th, Moon Libra

Neil Armstrong, 5th August 1930, 0.31am, Washington, OH, USA, Gemini Ascendant, Sun in 3rd, Moon Sagittarius

Arnold Schwarzenegger, 30th July 1947, 4.10am, Graz, Austria,

Cancer Ascendant, Sun in 1st, Moon Capricorn

Moon

Princess Margaret (UK), 21st August 1930, Glamis, Scotland, 9.22pm, Aries Ascendant, Sun in 5th, Moon Cancer

Houses

Steve Martin, 14th August 1945, Waco, TX, USA, 5.54am, Leo Ascendant, Sun in 1st, Moon Scorpio

Shelley Winters, 18th August 1920, Saint Louis, MO, USA, 0.05am, Gemini Ascendant, Sun in 3rd, Moon Libra

Amy Shapiro, 13th August 1951, 11.12pm, Boston, MA, USA, Taurus Ascendant, Sun in 4th, Moon Capricorn

Clara Bow, 29th July 1905, 8.20pm, Brooklyn (Kings County), New York, USA, Pisces Ascendant, Sun in 5th, Moon Cancer

Belinda Carlisle, 17th August 1958, 7.17pm, Los Angeles, CA, USA, Aquarius Ascendant, Sun in 7th, Moon Libra

Simon Bolivar, 24th July 1783, 10.34pm, Caracas, Venezuela, Aries Ascendant, Sun in 4th, Moon Gemini

Napoleon Bonaparte, 15th August 1769, 11.30am, Ajaccio, France, Scorpio Ascendant, Sun in 10th, Moon Capricorn

Bill Clinton, 19th August 1946, 8.51am, Hope, Arkansas, USA, Libra Ascendant, Sun in 11th, Moon Taurus

Monica Lewinsky, 23rd July 1973, 12.21pm, Libra Ascendant, Sun in 10th, Moon Taurus

Dodona Books offers a broad spectrum of divination systems to
suit all, including Astrology, Tarot, Runes, Ogham, Palmistry,
Dream Interpretation, Scrying, Dowsing, I Ching, Numerology,
Angels and Faeries, Tasseomancy and Introspection.